25 MEMORABLE MOMENTS FROM ENTER THE DRAGON

1) The Opening Scene: Bruce Lee's character, named Lee, is shown demonstrating his martial arts prowess in a sparring match.

2) Lee's Philosophy: "It's like a finger pointing away to the moon. Don't concentrate on the finger or you will miss all that heavenly glory."

3) Roper and Williams Intro: The introduction of John Saxon's character, Roper, and Jim Kelly's character, Williams, showcasing their skills.

4) Mirror Room Fight: Lee's fight in a maze of mirrors against the antagonist, Han, is one of the most visually striking sequences.

5) Lee's Scars: The revealing of the scratch marks on Lee's face and body, which serve as reminders of his sister's tragic death.

6) Guard Break: Lee's precise and methodical breaking of a guard's neck, showcasing his deadly efficiency.

7) The Flashback: The story of Lee's sister, Su Lin, her confrontation with O'Hara, and her tragic end.

8) Lee vs. O'Hara: Bruce Lee's fight against Bob Wall's character, O'Hara, culminating in O'Hara's death.

9) "Boards Don't Hit Back": Lee's iconic line after breaking a board with his fist during his fight against O'Hara.

10) Underground Discoveries: Lee's discovery of the underground drug operation on Han's island. Williams vs. Han: The battle where Williams takes on Han but is eventually defeated.

11) Roper's Refusal: Roper refuses to fight Lee, despite Han's insistence.

12) Snake Surprise: Lee uses a snake as a distraction while infiltrating the enemy's lair.

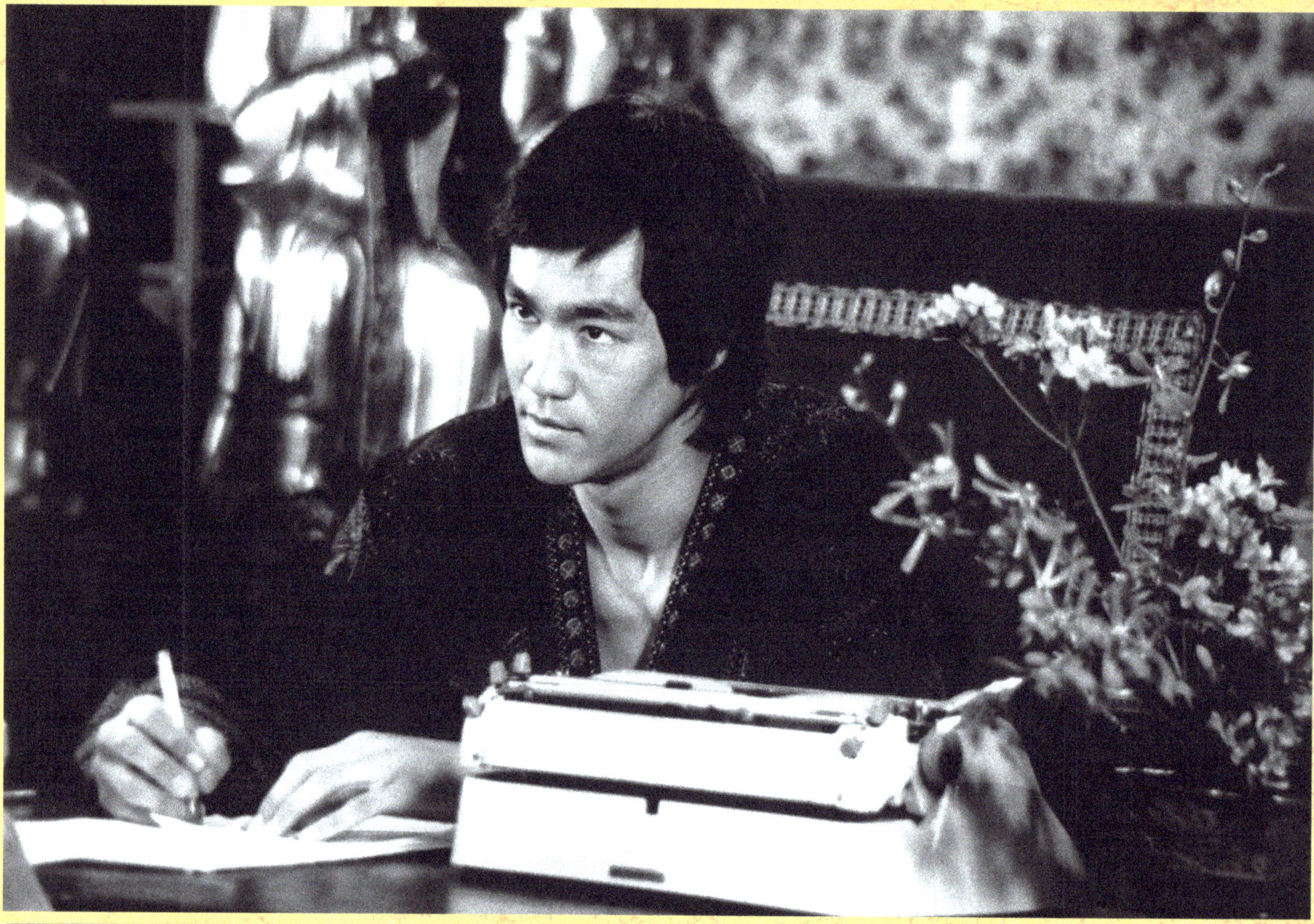

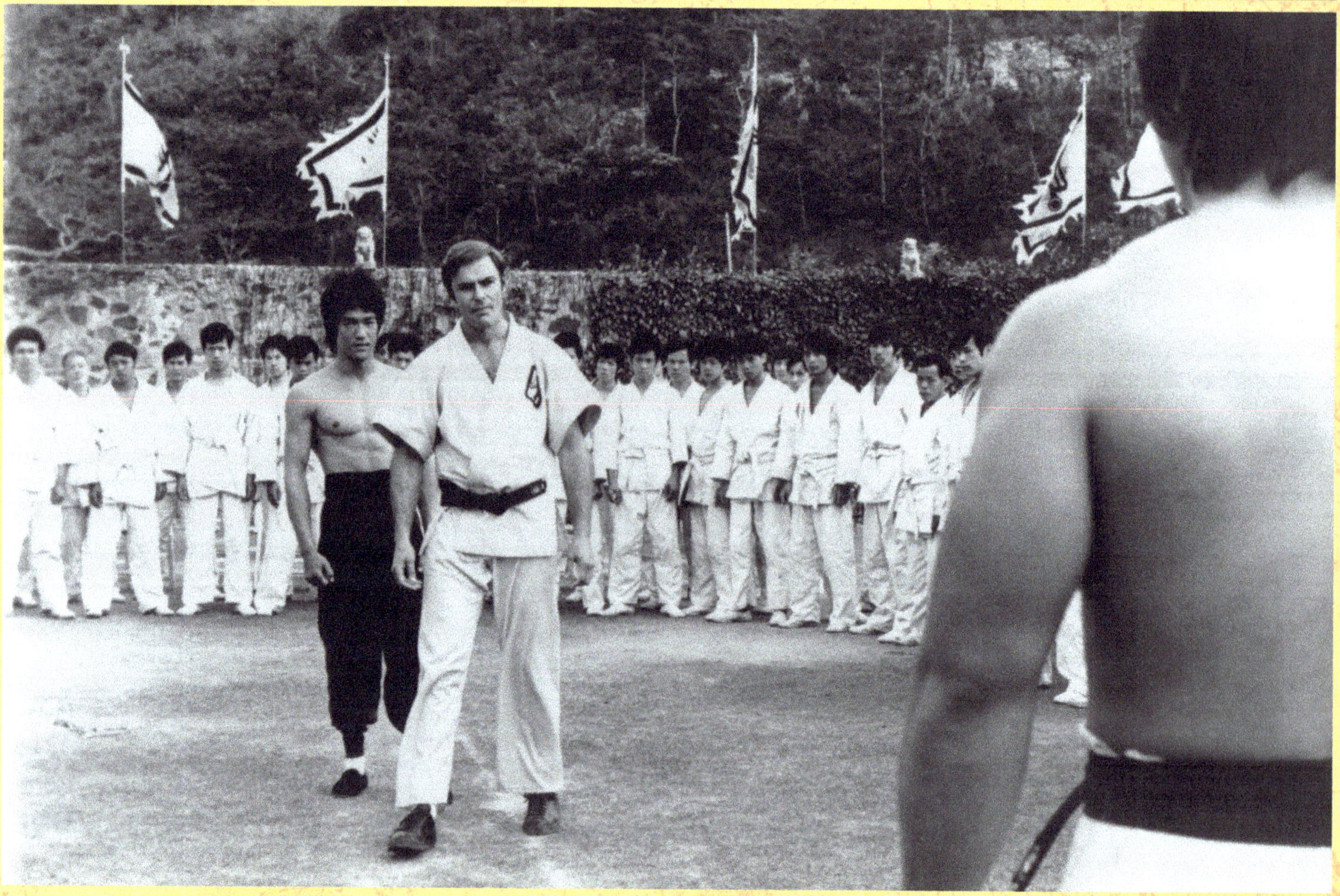

13) The Tournament Begins: The commencement of the martial arts tournament on Han's island, with fighters from all around the world.

14) Lee's Infiltration: Lee sneaking around the compound, showcasing his agility and stealth.

15) Bolo Fights: Bolo Yeung's character's brutal fights, displaying his immense strength.

16) The Hand with Claws: Han's metal-clawed hand becomes a symbol of his menacing presence.

17) Sound Strategy: Lee uses sound to mislead guards during his covert operations.

18) Roper's Gamble: Roper bets on Lee to win his fights, knowing his capabilities.

19) "You have offended my family and the Shaolin temple": Lee confronting Han about his criminal activities.

20) Mass Brawl: The large-scale fight that breaks out in the climax, with prisoners, guards, and the heroes clashing.

21) Roper vs. Bolo: Roper's intense battle against Bolo, the muscle-bound enforcer.

22) The Darts: Han's use of concealed darts as a weapon against Lee.

23) Rescue: Lee and Roper freeing the prisoners from their cells, leading to an uprising.

24) Lee's Victory: After a tense battle, Lee finally triumphs over Han, cementing his status as a legendary martial artist.

25) These moments are a testament to the film's unique blend of storytelling, martial arts choreography, and character development. "Enter the Dragon" remains a classic and an enduring legacy of Bruce Lee's talent and philosophy.

Eastern Heroes: Bruce Lee Special Vol.2 #3

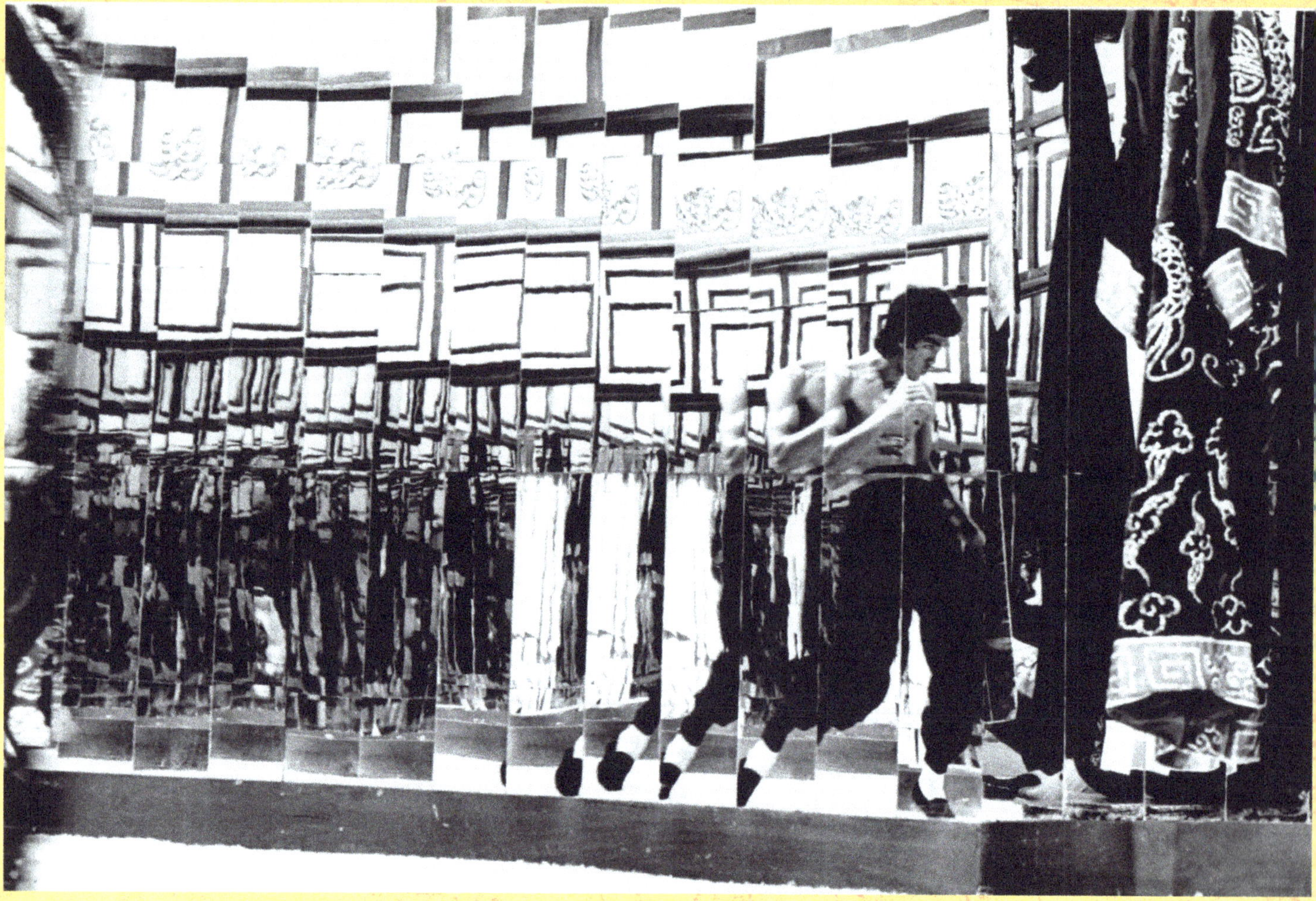

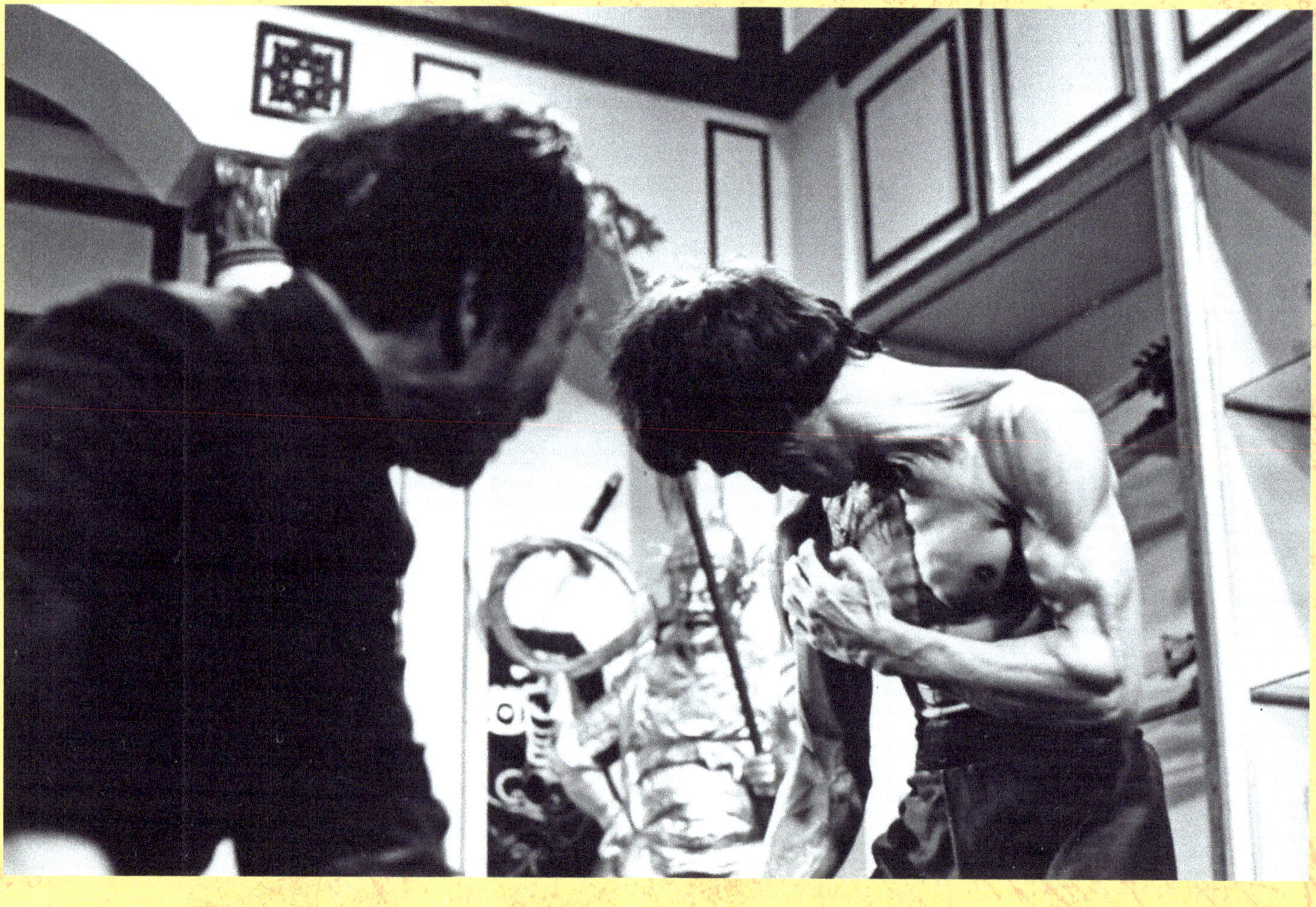

The Bruce Lee Column
BRUCE LEE BOOTLEGS
BY MICHAEL NESBITT

One of the major highlights for old-school collectors of Bruce Lee during the 1980s and 90s was collecting bootlegged VHS videos that were sold on the Black-Market. In these modern times, Bruce Lee collectors have an abundance of high-quality footage released on DVD, Blu-ray and 4K Ultra HD to choose from, especially the uncut versions of Bruce Lee movies. With the new release of The Bruce Lee at Golden Harvest box set by Arrow Films, this month The Bruce Lee Column, takes a look at the old-school pirated VHS videos.

New collectors of the genre may not know that before DVD was ever a thing, most of the fans would buy unlicensed pirated VHS video tapes on the Black Market. Long-time Bruce Lee collectors will adamantly tell you that these video pirates and the videos they sold were heroes, who supplied a lifeline for fans. For a long period of time, this was the only way to get uncut Bruce Lee movies, rare documentaries and never-before-seen footage.

For myself, living in the North-East of England in the mid to late 1980s, it was impossible to find any rare footage of Bruce Lee, and it was only when these Black-Market dealers of Asian action movies, started setting up mail order delivery services, that I was able to purchase these second, third or even fourth generation copied cassette tapes. At first, there were only a small number of companies set up for this exact purpose, the likes of; Eastern Heroes, (formally known as The Jackie Chan Fan Club); Eastern Entertainment and Tales from the East, were some of the best places to purchase these rarities. But the main company that ran the show was Shaolin Video, run by long-time Bruce Lee fan, Chris Alexis. Shaolin Video offered a huge back catalogue of titles, ranging from 1970s Shaw Brothers movies to the rarest of all Bruce Lee footage. Unfortunately for a lot of collectors, we had to pay top dollar for a pirated VHS cassette. Back when I first started collecting, VHS tapes would cost £28 each, and considering my first job was as a YTS (Youth Training Scheme), that was a full week's wage for me.

However, the expense of the cassettes failed in comparison to the excitement you would feel when you got that golden parcel delivered to your front door. I remember when I received my very first order, which was sometime in 1989. At the time, I had saved up a few pounds a week for nearly two months to be able to purchase two VHS cassettes. The first cassette was the original Chinese uncut version of Fist of Fury, which included the then-fabled nunchaku scenes. The second VHS tape I received, was a documentary-style video called; The Bruce Lee Souvenir. The Bruce Lee Souvenir was an amalgamation of different things collected on one cassette. The main part is the 10-minute documentary "Bruce Lee on Location Hong Kong", which was previously released on Super 8mm and 16mm, which showed rare behind-the-scenes footage of Bruce Lee from Enter the Dragon. Then there was the pilot episode of the Green Hornet TV series, starring Bruce Lee as Kato, called The Silent Gun. To finish off the cassette tape, there were various trailers for all of Bruce Lee's movies. To say that I loved these Black Market VHS tapes is a complete understatement, and I would watch them religiously over the next few years.

It wasn't just the cassettes and the covers that I loved, but also the catalogues that would arrive on the doorstep three to four times a year. And even though these were rudimentary black and white photocopies, these themselves would become highly collectable. Even though the price was high, it didn't deter me from purchasing many Black-Market VHS tapes from most of the companies that sold them. I remember getting a Donnie Yen 3 tape deal from Rick Baker at Eastern Heroes, which comprised of Tiger Cage, Mismatched Couple, and the fabulous Drunken Tai Chi. Another great deal I got from Eastern Heroes was volumes one and two of their trailer tape, which was comprised of 2-3 hours of Asian action movie trailers on each cassette. I can never find it in my heart to sell, or give these tapes away, and I still have both to this day. And God only knows how much money I spent with Eastern Entertainment. Cassette tapes were a little cheaper from them, and I must have bought hundreds of films over the space of a few years. The first ones I got from them included my first Jet Li movies; The Bodyguard from Beijing, and My Father the Hero. But for Bruce Lee footage, there was only one place to go, and that was Shaolin Video.

Shaolin Video was one of the first underground video dealers, which was started up by Chris Alexis in the mid-1980s. Chris had several contacts who would sell him Asian action movies, which he would then copy and resell on the Black-Market. At one point during the late 1980s, Chris had partnered up with Rick Baker to run the Jackie Chan Fan Club, which would later be refashioned into Eastern Heroes. After Chris and Rick parted ways in the early 1990s, Chris would go on to establish one of the best series of conventions Britain had ever seen, with his "Tracking the Dragon Bruce Lee Conventions." Bringing guests over such as Bob Baker from Fist of Fury; John Saxon and Jim Kelly from Enter the Dragon and a host of other actors and long-time students of Bruce Lee. Chris even started up the Bruce Lee and Friends Fan Club in the mid-1990s. However, by the millennium, Chris had completely disappeared from the scene. For most fans of the genre, Chris was instrumental in bringing some of the rarest Bruce Lee footage to VHS. With his many contacts in the Bruce Lee community, and having known and worked with former Bruce Lee students, family members, and actors who appeared with Bruce Lee on screen, Chris had managed to track down some of the most amazing Bruce Lee footage. Here are just a few examples of what Chris and Shaolin Video supplied to the fans.

The Big Boss , Fist of Fury , The Way of the Dragon , Enter the Dragon, Game of Death Remember in the 1980s and 90s these movies on VHS were cut, but Shaolin Video supplied the most uncut versions you could get.

The Green Hornet, Long Street, Here Comes the Brides, Batman, Ironside. Again back in the 80s and 90s, it was virtually impossible to get these TV series

featuring Bruce Lee.

Bruce Lee The Legend
I still consider this 1984 Bruce Lee documentary to be the best one released. Back in the day, it cost over £60 to buy the original VHS, as it was only available on rental, so to get one on the Black-Market was music to most fans' ears.

Bruce Lee and James Coburn Workout
Rare movie footage of Bruce Lee training James Coburn in his backyard with Bruce Lee himself narrating it.

Bruce Lee Wing Chun Demonstration
Rare footage of Bruce Lee teaching Wing Chun.

The World of Bruce Lee
A rare Japanese documentary on Bruce Lee. This documentary has some very rare, but really bad quality, black-and-white footage of Bruce Lee from behind-the-scenes of Game of Death.

Bruce Lee Japanese Home Movie
Another rare Japanese documentary on Bruce Lee. This tape includes rare footage of Bruce Lee working out in his backyard with Kareem Abdul-Jabbar, Dan Inosanto, Herb Jackson and others.

Bruce Lee Nunchaku in Action
This cassette featured the 8mm footage of Dan Inosanto using Nunchaku techniques that appeared in the book of the same name.

Bruce Lee The Screen Test
Bruce Lee's 1965 screen test for 20th Century Fox.

Bruce Lee The Canadian Interview
The 1971 Pierre Berton interview with Bruce Lee.

Bruce and Jacky Documentary
A rare Japanese documentary on Bruce Lee and Jackie Chan. This documentary includes rare footage of Bruce appearing on HKTV.

Legend of a Fighter
A fan-made Bruce Lee documentary.

Long Beach Internationals
Rare footage of Bruce Lee performing at Ed Parkers Long Beach Internationals.

Bruce Lee and Friends

An amalgamation of rare footage from other Bruce Lee VHS cassettes.

Bruce Lee Documentary
A fan-made three-hour documentary produced by Shaolin Video.

And then there are the Bruce Lee Conventions and Training Tapes.
The Tracking the Dragon Conventions.
The Way of the Intercepting Fist by Howard Williams.
The Power Punch by Howard Williams.
Bruce Lee's Basic Chi Sao by James DeMile.
Jeet Kune Do Training Vols 1-5 by Jerry Poteet.

You can keep your DVDs, Blu-rays, and Online Digital. For me and many other old-school collectors, there was no better feeling than the excitement you had finding a new VHS tape advertised in a Martial Arts Movie Catalogue, ordering it, waiting weeks, maybe even months for it to be delivered, and then, finally holding that fourth-generation, bad quality VHS cassette, with photocopied sleeve, in your hand and playing it on your massive VHS Video Recorder.

WAY OF THE INTERCEPTING FIST

Volume 1.

Bruce Lee

LONGSTREET

STERLING SILLIPHANT WROTE THIS EPISODE SPECIFICALLY WITH BRUCE LEE IN MIND — ALLOWING BRUCE TO DEMONSTRATE NOT ONLY HIS REVOLUTIONARY MARTIAL ARTS BUT ALSO HIS PHILOSOPHY

Bruce Lee in LONGSTREET

BRUCE LEE CLASSICS

Volume 1.

PAL VHS

BRUCE LEE'S LONGSTREET — THE LOST CLASSIC

WEDNESDAYS CHILD

I SEE SAID THE BLIND MAN

MORE EPISODES FROM THE HIGHLY ACCLAIMED SERIES — LEE'S PERFORMANCES IN EACH ARE OF THE HIGHEST QUALITY — DEMONSTRATING HIS ENORMOUS TALENT AS AN ACTOR AS WELL AS A CONSUMATE MARTIAL ARTIST

Volume 2.
Bruce Lee

LONGSTREET

Bruce Lee in LONGSTREET

BRUCE LEE CLASSICS

Volume 2.

PAL VHS

Eastern Heroes: Bruce Lee Special Vol.2 #3

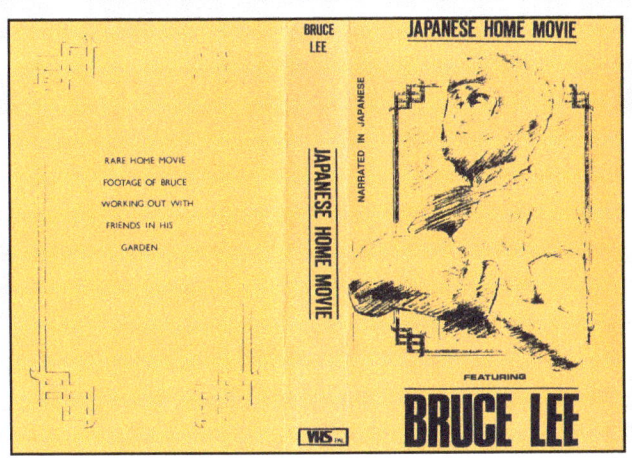

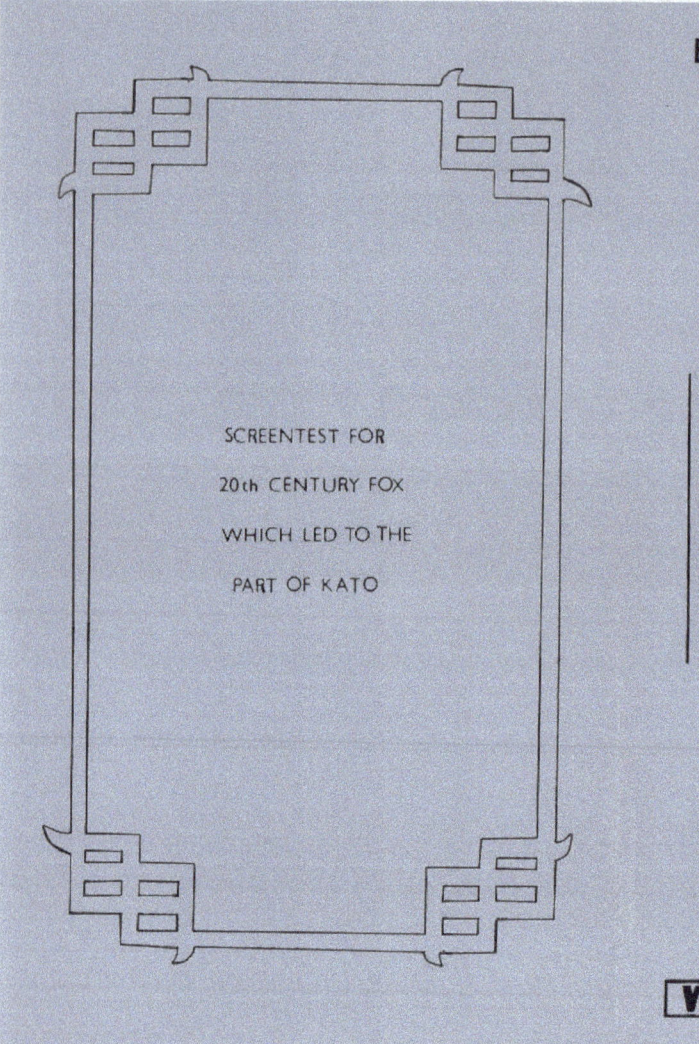

BRUCE and JACKIE
DOCUMENTARY

BRUCE AND JACKIE DOCUMENTARY

DRAGON Vs DRAGON
Running time 60 minutes.

This Documentary was made in Hong Kong Sereral yhears after the ultimely death of the ULTIMATE MARTIALARTIST - BRUCE LEE. Friends who knew him gave their opinion and a rare interview with one of his techers in Hong Kong. Sone rare footage of Bruce Lee demonstrrating his extraodinary skills on HKTV.
Soon after a new star was on the horison, a stuntman comedian and also a master of Kung Fu styles with a different approach named Jackie Chan. Jackie Chan in a rare interview shows off his acrobatis skills in a rare interview on roller skates in the USA. And talks about his mad stunts. Judge for yourself who is the true King Of Kung Fu.

BRUCE LEE COLLECTION

£25.00 each
plus £2.00 p+p each

£25.00 each

BEST QUALITY EVER!

THE NEW BRUCE LEE COLLECTION EXCLUSIVELY FROM SHAOLIN VIDEO
BEST OF BOTH WORLDS - CHINESE FIGHTING FOOTAGE, ENGLISH DIALOGUE - DYNAMITE QUALITY

THE NEW GENERATION
REMEMBER, WE SET THE STANDARDS. WE WILL BE SELLING THE 5 BRUCE LEE FILMS CALLED SIMPLY, THE NEW GENERATION. LASER QUALITY MASTERS, FULLY UNCUT.

WAY OF THE DRAGON
Complete uncut, laser quality master includes soup scene, double nunchukas, extended Cuck Norris fight scene, original war cries and sound effects. Sounds more realistic compared to USA and U.K. versions. Simply a dream come true. (All fights have chinese soundtrack.). Also original cover artwork, English version.

FIST OF FURY
Laser quality, complete uncut with nunchukas. All fights have original Chinese soundtrack. More realistic, again better than USA and U.K. version. Original artwork, English version.

BIG BOSS
Full uncut version. Extra footage chain fight scene. Extended fight at swimming pool with Bruce. Original soundtrack, original artwork. Collectors item.

GAME OF DEATH - 102 MIN
Note about Game of Death. This film has always been a problem. Indeed, making it wasn't exactly an easy task, as Bob Clause told me.
Mandarin version with subtitle nunchuka fight was cut from this version (Far East).
Cantonese version, no subs, was edited down many scenes and was shorter when measured. Surprisingly, the U.K. and USA version was the most complete, especially for dialogue, but the problem with this was the nunchuka fight with Dan Inosanto was cut and the fight in the greenhouse was cut with Billy Lo which later appeared in Game of Death 2. So we edited this master professionally. Now you can purchase Game of Death complete with ALL fights. English version but with Chinese soundtrack on all fights. Excellent quality.

ENTER THE DRAGON
A.K.A. OPERATION DRAGON
The New Generation. Complete uncut version. Again this version has had the same treatment, same quality laser with nunchukas, original Chinese soundtrack with Bruce Lee's battlecries, includes new scene, Bruce visiting the Monk.
ENGLISH DIALOGUE

For further details on our large selection of titles send to:

SHAOLIN VIDEO, P.O. Box 445, LONDON SW11 5QL

Please make cheques payable to Shaolin Videos • Allow 14 days for delivery.

• **FILM SHOW** •
Saturday, 24 May, 1992 • Hotel Ibis, London
Doors open 1.00p.m. • CRAZY FILM SALE: Videos from £5.00...Call 081 679903 for details

Eastern Heroes: Bruce Lee Special Vol.2 #3

SHAOLIN VIDEO ◆ SHAOLIN VIDEO ◆ SHAOLIN VIDEO

1 BLACK BELT JONES with Jim Kelly.
LIMITED. Cover signed by Jim Kelly.
CLASSIC. PRICE: £10 + £2 P&P

ENTER THE FAT DRAGON. Samo Hung. Subtitled £22 inc P&P

2 TATTOO CONNECTION with Jim Kelly.
LIMITED. Cover signed by Jim Kelly.
PRICE: £15 + £2 P&P

REBELLIOUS RIENG (English) £22 inc P&P

3 LAZER MISSION (Uncut)
with Brandon Lee. English Lang.
PRICE: £22 + £2 P&P

4 JKD VOL. 4:
5 WAYS OF ATTACK
PRICE: £20 + £2 P&P

JKD VOLS 1, 2, 3 ALSO AVAILABLE £22 inc P&P

5 JKD VOL. 5:
EQUIPMENT TRAINING By Jerry Poteet
PRICE: £20 + £2 P&P

HITMAN IN THE HAND OF BUDDHA £22 inc P&P

6 JKD FOR WOMEN NO. 6
PRICE: £20 + £2 P&P

7 BRUCE LEE: LEGEND OF A FIGHTER
The only documentary of Bruce that exists to date.
With J. Coburn; J. Saxon; B. Baker; Chuck Norris
Bruce Lee interview. 90 mins.
PRICE: £25 + £2 P&P

BRUCE LEE SOUVENIR TAPE: MAKING OF ENTER THE DRAGON £12 inc P&P

8 LONG BEACH INTERNATIONAL
Rare, Colour /Black & White footage. Approx. 50 mins.
Bruce Lee was discovered for his talent at this tournament.
No sound of 8mm cini transfer. A MUST!
PRICE: £25 + £2 P&P

3 EPISODES THE GREEN HORNET £22 EACH inc P&P

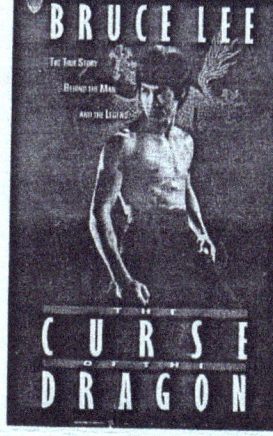

DOCUMENTARY USA
PRICE: £25 + £2 P&P
Video by Fred Weintraub

£12 inc P&P

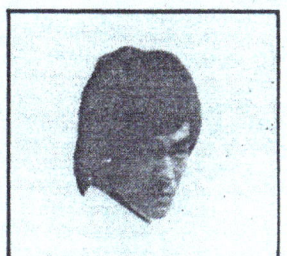

10 BRUCE LEE PHOTO
Taken by John Saxon on set
of Enger The Dragon.
Official Tribute

Shaolin Video

PO BOX 445, LONDON SW11 5QL.
TEL/FAX: 0181 679 9033

BRUCE LEE - LEGEND OF A FIGHTER (SPECIAL EDITION) - £20

BRUCE LEE - ENTER THE DRAGON (SUBTITLES) - £15

BRUCE LEE - JKD VOLUMES 1 - 6 - £20 EACH

THE GREEN HORNET - VOL 1, 2 & 3, 8 TO 9 EPISODES EACH - £20 EACH

THE GREEN HORNET - 1 HOUR DOCUMENTARY - £15

BRUCE LEE - GAME OF DEATH 2 - £15

BRUCE LEE THE MAN & THE LEGEND (DIGITAL REMASTER) - £20

BRUCE LEE - THE BIOGRAPHY (1 Hr DOCUMENTARY INC. RARE FOOTAGE) - £20

BRUCE LEE - THE WAY OF THE DRAGON (SUBTITLES & BRUCE VOICEOVER) - £14

BRUCE LEE - HERE COMES THE BRIDES (BRUCE CAMEO APPEARANCE) - £15

BRUCE LEE - PHOTO STORY VOL.1 & 2 (BOTH APROX. 3 Hrs.) - £20 EACH

BRUCE LEE NUNCHUKAS BY DAN INOSANTO (FILMED ON SUPER 8) - £15

BRUCE LEE - THE BIG BOSS (CANTONESE/NO SUBTITLES) - £15

THE BRANDON LEE TAPES (30 MINS OF RARE FOOTAGE) - £15

BRANDON LEE - OUT OF THE SHADOW (INTERVIEWS & FOOTAGE) - £20

SHANNON LEE - ENTER THE PHOENIX (EXC. UK INTERVIEW) - £20
* Limited Signed 10 by 8 B/w photo - £10

ENTER THE FAT DRAGON - WITH SAMO HAUNG, (SUBTITLED) - £15

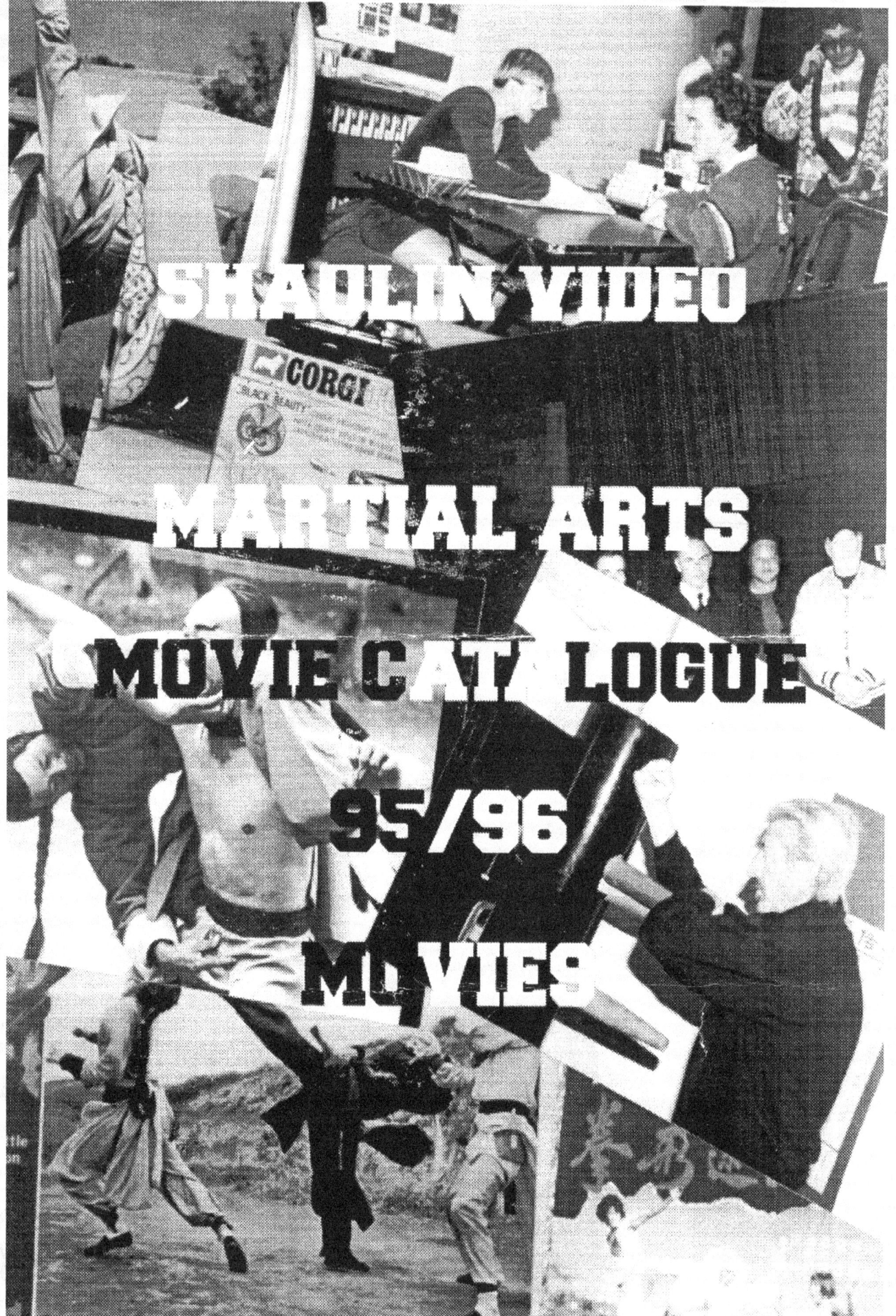

MARTIAL ARTS FILMS

STILLS AND PHOTOGRAPHS OF MOST OF YOUR FAVORITE STARS ARE AVAILABLE ON REQUEST FROM SHAOLIN PHOTO UK. SAME ADDRESS AS ON FRONT PAGE OF CATALAGUE.

BRUCE LEE PHOTOS NEVER BEFORE SEEN.
JACKY CHAN STILLS FROM HIS MOVIES AND OFF CAMERA SHOTS, ALSO HWANG JANG LEE JOEN LUI, PATTY SAMO AND MANY MORE. COLOR/B&W 6x8½ 10x8 GLOSSY

EVERY MARTIAL ARTS FILM AVAILABLE IN THE U.K. CAN NOW BE PURCHASED FROM US

NEW ADDRESS IS

61 COTTON HOUSE
NEW PARK ROAD
LONDON SW2 4LA

E (english speaking)   SB (shaw brothers production)

SUB (chinese language with english subtitle)   UNCUT (complete original)

NO SUB (chinese language with no subtitle)

PLEASE NOTE

ALL FILMS £22.00 (including postage & package)   FILMS MARKED WITH * £25.00

SHAOLIN VS NINJA — ALEXANDER LOU

SHAOLIN CHASTITY KF — ALAN HSU

SHAOLIN VS LAMA — GEORGE CHANG

- SV01: ONE ARM BOXER (E) WANG YU (UNCUT VERSION)
- SV02: THE SWORD (E) (UNCUT)
- *SV03: ABOVE THE LAW (E) (UNCUT)
- SV04: TWO GREAT CAVAIERS (SUB)
- SV05: 7 GRAND MASTERS (E) (UNCUT VERSION)
- SV06: WARRIOR FROM SHAOLIN AKA CARPONE (SUB)
- SV07: THE HIMUAYAN (E) (UNCUT) HIMALAYAN (FLASH LEGS)
- SV08: BORN INVINCIBLE (E) (SUB) (UNCUT VERSION)
- *SV09: RETURN OF THE DRAGON (UNCUT) WITH NUNCHU BRUCE LEE
- SV10: WHEN TEAK WANDO STRIKE (E) (UNCUT)
- *SV11: FIST OF FURY (E) (UNCUT) WITH NUNCHU
- SV12: LAST HURRAY FOR SHIVARY (E) (UNCUT)
- SV13: FIVE DEADLY VENOMS (E) (UNCUT)
- SV14: HOLY ROBE OF SHAOLIN (NO SUB)
- SV15: SHANG HI 13 (E) (SUB) 13 STARS
- SV16: SNUFF BOTTLE CONNECTION (E) (SUB)
- SV17: FATE OF LEE KHAN (E) (UNCUT)
- SV18: MAGIC CRYSTAL (E) (SUB)
- SV19: IRON MONKEY (SUB) (UNCUT) CHEN KWAN TAI
- SV20: AVENGING EAGLE (E) (UNCUT) TI LUNG
- SV21: WAY OF THE DRAGON (E) BRUCE LEE
- SV22: KING OF THE RING (E) ANTOI ANOKI & BENNY THE JET
- SV23: DEATH DUEL OF KUNG FU (NO SUB)

DEATH DUEL OF MANTIS
Starring CHIN YIN FEI, TING YUEN CHIN
"A divish period drama with novel martial arts, it highlights some of the most off-beat and bizarre Kung Fu acrobatics since Jacky Chan's Drunken Master" style unique unusual and imaginative.

Shaolin Video

Martial Arts
Mail
Order
Movies

SHAOLIN VIDEO

SHAOLIN VIDEO

Martial Arts Christmas specials Movies

EASTERN ENTERTAINMENT
(0850) 976186

PO BOX 26, LEEDS, WEST YORKSHIRE,
LS25 7XE, ENGLAND, UNITED KINGDOM.

August 1999 edition

EASTERN ENTERTAINMENT

The definitive A-Z of Hong Kong cinema
from the classic days right up until today

PLEASE QUOTE CODES WHEN ORDERING

See latest updates for
prices and special offers

SHANQUIA SHANQUIA AVAILABLE....

MERCHANDISE UPDATE

DONNIE YEN COLLECTION ~ A DRAGON DESCOVERED ~

Rising star, and the face of the '90's **DONNIE YEN** is following the success of 'IN THE LINE OF DUTY'.
We are offering you THREE more DONNIE MOVIES, (Imports) with the standard of action and stunts that you're only used to seeing in JACKIE CHAN movies.
'SAY YOU SAW THEM FIRST' ALL VERSIONS UNCUT !!

£16.95 each
+£1.40 P+P
ALL THREE £45.00
FREE P+P

TIGER CAGE
Brutal Action
Extra Footage Not
Seen in Cinema Print

DRUNKEN TAI CHI
Uncut English Version
In the same Vain as
Drunken Master.

MISMATCHED COUPLES
Subtitled
Break Dancing, Foot Kicking
Hi-Action

FREE DONNIE YEN BASEBALL CAP WITH EACH ORDER !

ACTION ! ACTION ! ACTION !
FEMME FATALE ACTION 2
MORE LADIES ON THE BEAT !

ALSO AVAILABLE ROBO FORCE, a cross between Robo Cop, Die Hard and Total Recal! (Not Boxed) This movie was previewed on The Incredibly Strange Picture Show and has a Femme Fatale Robot on the warpath. FIVE STAR RATING***** UNCUT SUBTITLED
NOT TO BE MISSED !!!!

IN THE LINE OF DUTY 5
The Action Continues

OPERATION PINK SQUAD
£20.00

ANGEL 3
Moon Lee
Bad-Fast-&
Beautiful
Subtitled
£20.00

ULTRA FORCE
English Uncut
Import (A.K.A.
Police Assassins)
£20.00

MAGIC CRYSTAL
Cynthia Rothrock,
Richard Norton,
Andy Lau,
Magic Action.
£20.00

CYNTHIA KHAN
Subtitled
£20.00

MERCHANDISE CATALOGUE

ESTABLISHED NOVEMBER 1988

The Number 1 catalogue for collectors of ACTION MEMORABILIA IN EUROPE !

With more and more people collecting Action memorabilia, we are extending our catalogue all the time to cater for the high demand......and we are constantly trying to improve on the quality and service that we offer.

Your support in ordering through this catalogue helps us in our quest to bring you more information on all your favourite stars. (Which are all in **Eastern Heroes Magazine**).

We also hold cinema events and seminars along with our successful Roadshows, where you can actually meet your favourite stars in person! We have already brought you over the years and months, **Cynthia Rothrock, Donnie Yen, Loren Avondon, Mark Houghton, Gordon Lui (Lau Ka Fei), Vyncent Lynn.**

So support Eastern Heroes, because we are here for YOU !

' T ' SHIRTS

Hong Kong's most famous TRIO, all on one T shirt !

JACKIE CHAN, SAMO HUNG and YEUN BIAO

in **FULL GLORIOUS COLOUR**

LIMITED EDITION

A true collectors item ! M, L, XL, Sizes

ONLY

£5.95

FREE P+P Allow 14 days delivery.

MERCHANDISE UPDATE 2
THE JACKIE CHAN COLLECTION
Special collection of imported..... unedited versions.....containing footage unavailable in the UK...
A MUST FOR ALL JACKIE FANS   £20.00 EACH (ANY THREE £50.00) + £1.40 P+P

FEARLESS HYENA
SPECIAL UNCUT EDIT
(SUBTITLED)

SPIRITUAL KUNG-FU
Full cantonese version
subtitled

POLICE STORY
Over 20mins of extra footage, unavailable in UK print...(sub)

HALF A LOAF OF KUNG FU
Special Edit / Subtitled

THE PROTECTOR
Special Edit / Contains extra footage never seen in UK print (Chinese only)

NEW FIST OF FURY
Special Edition
Contains Jackie's
Nunchaka fight scene
English Version

36 WOOD MEN
Completely uncut
with extra footage
Cantonese/ English sub's

DRAGON FIST
Subtitled / uncut

CLASSIC FIGHT ACTION

All films £1.40 P+P

DIRTY HO
Gordon Lui / Wong Yu
Superb Action (sub)
£15.00

HIT MAN IN THE HAND OF BUDDAH
Hwang Jang Lee / Super foot fighting action
£17.95 / English

FISTFUL OF TALONS
Billy Chong/ Whang- In-Sik
ONE OF THE BEST MOVIES EVER!
£17.95 English

THE WARRIOR FROM SHAOLIN
Gordon Lui £20.00 subtitled
HIGHLY RECOMMENDED

Eastern Heroes: Bruce Lee Special Vol.2 #3

EASTERN HEROES

TOP H.K. MOVIE STARS

TOP FILMS!

TOP QUALITY

MERCHANDISING UPDATE SPRING 1993

ORDERING INFORMATION

All video orders will be delivered within **14 Days** from receipt of order (allow 2 days for order to reach us). If we don't supply on time then you can select any film of your choice *free*. In a new move to improve our mail order service, we are making this unbelieveable offer, to ensure that when you order your films you order from us and put the offer to the test. Just remember to date your order when sending and we will rush your film out a.s.a.p. (Please note if ordering on a Friday, date it for the Monday). ("(Sub)" denotes English subtitles, "E" English Language)

PLUS if you are looking for a particular video title send us a s.a.e. and in return we will try and locate the title for you. **THIS IS A FREE SERVICE**.

New titles coming in every week. Send s.a.e. for update...

*(All films are reproduction copies, boxed with colour sleeve)

New laserdisc versions are of the highest quality (60% better than VHS). Most titles selected in this new catalogue have been chosen for their quality. If you have any problems please return to address listed for immediate exchange.

- All titles **£18.00** each (special offer)
- Any 3 for **£50.00**
- **Postage & packing** £1.40 for the first film and then 50p for each film thereafter. Orders of £100.00 or more, free p&p

P.O. BOX 409, LONDON, SE18 3DW

LIMITED COLLECTOR'S VIDEO CATALOGUE
SUMMER 1994

FUTURE SHOP, 3A BUCK STREET, CAMDEN TOWN, LONDON, N1

NEW RELEASES

ALL TAPES ARE 100% ORIGINALS, AUTHORISED THROUGH ATV AND ARE IN CANTONESE LANGUAGE WITH ENGLISH SUBTITLES AND ARE ALL BBFC CERTIFICATED.

£18.00 EACH + £1.50 p&p (50p per title thereafter)

FONG SAI YUK 1 & 2
JET LEE once again delves into traditional Chinese folk lore bringing the legend alive with plenty of well choreographed fight scenes and some top notch comedy.
'15' CERT

KING OF BEGGARS ATV 1
CHOW SING CHI Blend of comedy and action as Chow goes traditional!!
'15'

ONCE UPON A TIME IN CHINA 2
JET LEE revives the Wong Fei Hung legend with an epic seque. Plenty of action and historical intrigue. '15'

IRON MONKEY
YU RONG KWONG fights foot to fist with DONNIE YEN in an fast paced traditional actioner, which takes as its source the Chinese version of Robin Hood. One of the best martial arts films of 1993.
ATV6 '15' CERT

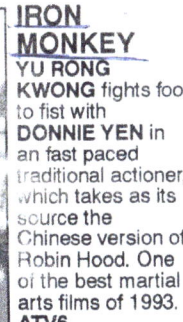

LOVE ON DELIVERY
CHOW SING CHI comedy which combines slapstick humour with high flying action as he takes on a Judo master in order to win the love of a woman. To find out how Ultraman and Garfield the cat figures in all this you'll have to watch and see!! Chinese New Year blockbuster.
ATV7 '15' CERT

CITY HUNTER ATV5 '15' CERT
JACKIE CHAN goes manga in motion as top crimefighter Ryu Saeba, foiling the attempts of a gang of terrorists to take over a pleasure cruiser. With Joey Wong, a host of battling babes and the cast of Streetfighter 2!!! Also starring the delicious Chingamy Yau.

TITLES AVAILABLE SOON – 1st AUG
FIRST SHOT Heroic Bloodshed with Ti Lung, Simon Yam and Waise Lee **ATV8** '18' CERT
ONCE UPON A TIME IN CHINA 3 The saga continues with Jet Lee **ATV9** '15' CERT
COMING SOON – WING CHUN
For further release details please write with s.a.e.

No Bruce (young) films

EASTERN HEROES
SPRING 1995 CATALOGUE

FUTURE SHOP, 3A BUCK STREET, CAMDEN TOWN, LONDON, NW1 8NJ

NEVER COMING TO A CINEMA OR TV STATION NEAR YOU!!! ONLY AVAILABLE ON VIDEO

EASTERN HEROES VIDEO TITLES
ALL TAPES ARE 100% ORIGINALS AND ARE IN CANTONESE LANGUAGE WITH ENGLISH SUBTITLES

£12.99 EACH (free p&p) - £1.00 off R.R.P.

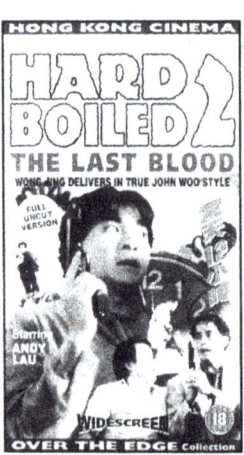

HARD BOILED 2: THE LAST BLOOD
ANDY LAU, ALAN TAM
Hi-octane Bloodshed action. A hospital besieged by terrorists and three heroes with an unlimited supply of bullets!!
WIDESCREEN
Cert '18'
EH0001

SPOOKY ENCOUNTERS
SAMO HUNG, LAM CHING YING
More high-powered ghostly goings on in the sequel to Encounter of the Spooky Kind.
Cert '15'
EH0003

DEADLY CHINA DOLLS
SIBELLE HU
All out femme fatale action as three battling babes take on a forgery gang.
WIDESCREEN with re-mastered subtitles
Cert '18'
EH0006
March 13th '95.

HOLY VIRGIN VS THE EVIL DEAD
DONNIE YEN
A blend of Category III eroticism, spooky shenanigans and martial arts action.
WIDESCREEN
Cert '18'
EH0002

MAGIC COP
LAM CHING YING, MICHIKO
MR VAMPIRE 5 as Lam Ching Ying takes on an evil spirit in modern day Hong Kong.
Cert 'PG'
EH0005

LETHAL PANTHER
YUKARI OSHIMA
Yukari swings into action in a 90 minute bulletfest
Cert '15'
EH0004

Eastern Heroes: Bruce Lee Special Vol.2 #3

HOLLYWOOD EAST VIDEO 電影

COLLECTORS CATALOGUE SPRING 1994

P.O. BOX 409, LONDON, SE18 3DW

MODERN KUNG FU

FONG SAI YUK 1
Jet Lee
A must see!! (Cant/Subs) TW268

FONG SAI YUK 2
Jet Lee. Available Now!!!
(Subs) TW269

THE FLYING FOX
Lai Ming. Top notch new action film
(Man/Subs) TW270

ONCE UPON A TIME IN CHINA 4
Wong Fei Hung action
(Man/Subs) TW271

KUNG FU CULT HERO
Jet Lee, Samo Hung
(Subs) TW272

THE EAGLE SHOOTING HERO
Jackie Cheung. Wild action.
(Cant/Subs) TW273

PRODIGAL PIRATES
Wong Fai Hung re-make. Conan Lee.
(Man/Subs) TW274

LIQUID SWORD 2
Aaron Kwok, Lau Gar Fei & all star cast action (Subs) TW275

THE ASSASSIN
Mok Sui Cheung. Superb new period piece (Man/Subs) TW276

IRON MONKEY
Donnie Yen
(Man/Subs) TW277

BUTTERFLY AND SWORD
Donnie Yen, Michelle Yeoh fantasy swordplay (Cant/Subs) TW278

THE SINGING KILLER
Ti Lung, David Chiang
(Man/Subs) TW279

BLADE OF FURY
Samo Hung, Ti Lung
Best film 1994 (Cant/Subs) TW280

SWORD STAINED WITH ROYAL BLOOD
Yuen Biao re-make of Shaw Bros classic (Subs) TW281

TAI CHI MASTER
Excellent Jet Lee drama
(Subs) TW282

電影 HONG KONG VIDEO
COLLECTORS CATALOGUE
SUMMER 1994 — P.O. BOX 409, LONDON, SE18 3DW

CLASSICS YOU MAY HAVE MISSED

PROJECT S (POLICE STORY 3 – PART 2)
Michelle Yeoh, Yu Rong Kwong, Jackie Chan. New subtitled print. Highly recommended. (Cant/Subs) **TW330**

FIRST SHOT
Ti Lung, Maggie Cheung, Simon Yam, Waise Lee. Excellent all cast starrer in this first rate Heroic Bloodshed movie. If you enjoyed A BETTER TOMORROW then this is a must. (Man/Subs) **TW331**

HOT HOT & POM POM
Lam Chin Ying, Jackie Cheung. Explosive Heroic Bloodshed action with the ultimate hi-octane ending. (Cant/Subs) **TW332**

FUTURE COPS
All-star cast headed by Andy Lau. Streetfighter II action. Excellent. (Man/Subs) **TW333**

EASTERN CONDORS
Now for the first time in English. Still one of the best action films to come out of Hong Kong (Eng) **TW334**

HEIST (GOOD THE BAD & THE BEAUTY)
Frankie Chan and the lovely Cherrie Cheung covort in this fast fighting modern day action flick with explosive stunts (Eng) **TW335**

CRIME STORY
Jackie Chan. Hard-hitting drama in the POLICE STORY fashion. Full uncut version. (Subs) **TW336**

POLICE STORY 3: SUPER COP
Jackie Chan, Michelle Khan. Breathtaking fight action is well balanced with the usual stunt mania! Classic Chan, now available in English, uncut & widescreen **TW337**

MERCHANDISE LIST

JACKIE PORTRAIT BY DEAN JONES FROM ISSUE NO. 7	£ 1.00 EACH
NEWSLETTER BACK ISSUES 1, 2, 3 (ONLY ONE PER PERSON) INCLUDING FOLDER	£ 8.00 PER SET
BIG BRAWL POSTER (SPECIAL OFFER) WERE £2.95 EACH SCALA CINEMA POSTER (SPECIAL OFFER) NOW ONLY	£ 1.50 EACH
J.C. FOLDER (SPECIAL OFFER) WAS £2.95 NOW (ONLY ONE PER PERSON)	£ 2.00
J.C. NEWSLETTER NO. 4 (16 PAGE B/W INCL. MIRACLE REVIEW/HAND OF DEATH)	£ 2.50
AUDIO SOUNDTRACKS - YOUNG MASTER / PROTECTOR / BIG BRAWL / ARMOUR OF GOD SPECIAL XMAS OFFER ALL FOUR FOR	£ 5.00 / £ 5.00 / £ 5.00 / £ 5.00 £18.00
THE PROTECTOR - LIMITED POSTER, FULL COLOUR A2. PICTURE SHOWS MULTIPLE SHOTS	£ 2.50
ARMOUR OF GOD - LIMITED POSTER, FULL COLOUR A2. JACKIE WITH CROSSBOW.	£ 2.50
FEARLESS HYENA PART II (ENGLISH)	£19.95
SPIRITUAL KUNG FU	£19.95
CHAN BEHIND THE SCENES VIDEO DOCUMENTARY (60 MINS APPROX) 1 HOUR	£20.00
HAND OF DEATH VIDEO - ENGLISH VERSION	£25.00
NEW POSTER, A3 COLOUR, MIRACLE	£ 5.00
BRUCE LEE TRANSFERS - SET OF 6 DIFFERENT POSES, FULL SIZE FOR T/SHIRTS. LIMITED.	PER £ 4.95 SET

WE ALSO HAVE A RANGE OF STILLS, FULL COLOUR, LAMINATED, A3 SIZE. UNFORTUNATELY, WE DO NOT HAVE SPACE TO SHOW YOU THE PICTURES BUT A DESCRIPTION IS OFFERED TO HELP YOU CHOOSE. STILLS ARE LIMITED AND COST £7.50 EACH.   ALL STILLS ARE EXCEPTIONALLY RARE.

PAINTED FACES - STILL SHOWS POSTER ADVERTISEMENT
EASTERN CONDORS - STILL SHOWS POSTER ADVERTISEMENT
HALF A LOAF OF KUNG FU - MULTI SHOTS FROM MOVIE
REVENGE OF DRUNKEN MASTER - POSTER ADVERT, JACKIE WITH VASE
REVENGE OF DRUNKEN MASTER - SYNOPSIS + PHOTOS
FILM SHOW POSTER, NOV 27TH 1988. ARTWORK BY DEAN JONES. SUPERB COLOUR ILLUSTRATION - EASTERN CONDORS, PROJECT A II, DRAGONS FOREVER.
THE PROTECTOR - AMERICAN POSTER WITH PHOTOGRAPHIC PICTURES
SNAKE IN EAGLES SHADOW - JACKIE
SNAKE IN EAGLES SHADOW - JACKIE IN TRAINING
SNAKE IN EAGLES SHADOW - JACKIE IN BATTLE
DRAGON LORD - JACKIE CLIMBING HUMAN PYRAMID
JACKIE 1 - A2 FULL COLOUR POSTER - JACKIE IN HALF BODY SHOT IN KUNG FU POSE - £5.00
JACKIE 2 - A2 FULL COLOUR POSTER - JACKIE IN SECOND HALF BODY SHOT - £5.00

PLEASE ALLOW 28 DAYS WHEN ORDERING, AS IF A PRODUCT SELLS OUT, WE DO TRY TO RE-ORDER SO AS NOT TO DISAPPOINT.

PLEASE ADD 75P POSTAGE AND PACKING TO ALL ORDERS FOR STILLS AND AUDIO CASSETTES, £1.00 PER VIDEO. POSTERS A2 SIZE FREE P+P.

NAME ....   ADDRESS ....

MEMBERSHIP NO. ....

DATE ORDERED ....

PLEASE SEND ORDERS TO:- J.C.F.C., MAIL ORDER, 15-17 FALCON RD., LONDON. SW11 2JP.

JACKIE CHAN MERCHANDISE LIST

MERCHANDISE LIST

JACKIE PORTRAIT BY DEAN JONES FROM ISSUE NO. 7	£1.00 EACH
NEWSLETTER BACK ISSUES 1, 2, 3 (ONLY ONE PER PERSON) INCLUDING FOLDER	£8.00 PER SET
BIG BRAWL POSTER (SPECIAL OFFER) WERE £2.95 EACH SCALA CINEMA POSTER (SPECIAL OFFER) NOW ONLY	£1.50 EACH
J.C. FOLDER (SPECIAL OFFER) WAS £2.95 NOW (ONLY ONE PER PERSON)	£2.00
J.C. NEWSLETTER NO. 4 (16 PAGE B/W INCL. MIRACLE REVIEW/HAND OF DEATH) + NO 5 (£2.50)	£2.50
AUDIO SOUNDTRACKS - YOUNG MASTER	£5.00
PROTECTOR	£5.00
BIG BRAWL	£5.00
ARMOUR OF GOD	£5.00
SPECIAL XMAS OFFER - ALL FOUR FOR	£18.00
THE PROTECTOR - LIMITED POSTER, FULL COLOUR A2. PICTURE SHOWS MULTIPLE SHOTS	£2.50
ARMOUR OF GOD - LIMITED POSTER, FULL COLOUR JACKIE WITH CROSSBOW.	£2.50
FEARLESS HYENA PART II (ENGLISH)	£19.95
SPIRITUAL KUNG FU	£19.95
CHAN BEHIND THE SCENES VIDEO DOCUMENTARY (60 MINS APPROX) 1 HOUR	£20.00
HAND OF DEATH VIDEO - ENGLISH VERSION	£20.00
NEW POSTER, A3 COLOUR, MIRACLE /SOLD OUT/	£5.00
BRUCE LEE TRANSFERS - SET OF 5 DIFFERENT POSES. FULL SIZE FOR T/SHIRTS. LIMITED.	£4.95 PER SET

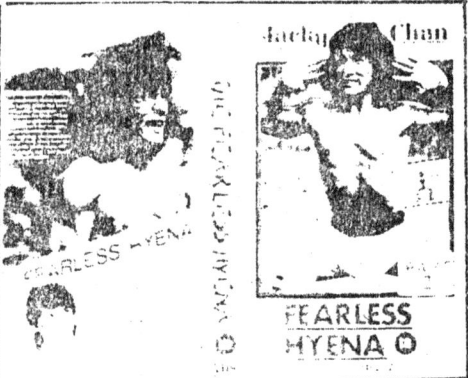

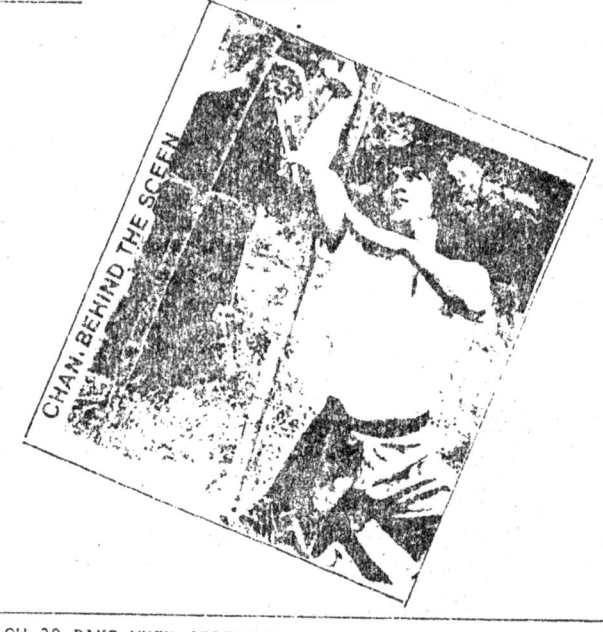

PLEASE ALLOW 28 DAYS WHEN ORDERING, AS IF A PRODUCT SELLS OUT, WE DO TRY TO RE-ORDER SO AS NOT TO DISAPPOINT.

PLEASE ADD 75P POSTAGE AND PACKING TO ALL ORDERS FOR STILLS AND AUDIO CASSETTES, £1.00 PER VIDEO. POSTERS A2 SIZE FREE P+P.

NAME .... ADDRESS ....

MEMBERSHIP NO ....

DATE ORDERED ....

PLEASE SEND ORDERS TO:- J.C.F.C., MAIL ORDER, 15-17 FALCON RD., LONDON. SW11 2JP.

Enter The Clones Of BRUCE

Synopsis

When Bruce Lee died in 1974 at the peak of his superstardom, he had completed only four feature films. But within hours of his funeral, Hong Kong movie studios began to produce hundreds of unauthorized biopics, sequels, prequels, spin-offs, and rip-offs starring a competing series of Lee lookalikes. Over the next decade, fueled by both deception and demand, 'Bruceploitation' would become a staple of global cinema.

Director **David Gregory** – who'd previously explored film's transgressive edges in his award-winning documentaries LOST SOUL: THE DOOMED JOURNEY OF RICHARD STANLEY'S ISLAND OF DR. MOREAU and BLOOD & FLESH: THE REEL LIFE & GHASTLY DEATH OF AL ADAMSON – now examines this uniquely '70s phenomenon via interviews with **Bruce Li, Bruce Le, Bruce Liang** and **Dragon Lee**; martial arts movie legends that include **Angela Mao, David Chiang, Phillip Ko, Casanova Wong, Yasuaki Kurata** and **Sammo Hung**; and the producers, directors, distributors and experts – along with copious clips from the films themselves – that for the first time reveal the history, controversy and legacy behind one of the most bizarre and successful genres in movie history.

The Production

"This is the first documentary I've done in which I didn't know much about the subject when I began developing it," says director **David Gregory** of ENTER THE CLONES OF BRUCE. "Few people do. But I'd been curious about these movies since seeing the box covers in video stores when I was a kid. That curiosity was reignited when Severin Films produced the Blu-ray compilation KUNG FU TRAILERS OF FURY. Clearly these actors' real names weren't 'Bruce Le', 'Bruce Li' or even 'Bruce Rhee', and hundreds of films couldn't be simply dismissed as 'Bruce Lee rip-off movies'. How did this sub-genre develop? Why was it so pervasive? How did these performers feel about being impersonators? No one had ever told the complete story of Bruceploitation."

Beginning in 2017, Gregory and his production team conducted more than thirty interviews across seven countries, tracking down the actors, producers, directors and distributors who created a phenomenon in which imitation became the sincerest form of profitability. Many of the principals, now in their 70s, speak candidly about their experiences for the first time. "What became most fascinating to me were the mixed feelings about how Bruceploitation had defined their careers," says Gregory. "They were all great admirers of Bruce Lee. Their intentions were for the most part honorable. But as one interviewee put it, they were making money from a ghost. And Lee's ghost remains potent."

There was also a strong element of archaeology to the production, as many Bruceploitation films were frequently recut and retitled by producers and distributors who also indiscriminately changed the lead actors' names. "There are unique nuances to many of these performers who would find ways to express their individuality," says Gregory. "And as the genre progressed, the films themselves got increasingly stranger and more entertaining. Bruceploitation has a richness that is constantly surprising."

Ultimately, ENTER THE CLONES OF BRUCE asks audiences to consider the power of iconography and the role it plays in keeping our legends alive. "Bruce Lee is as much an icon as Marilyn Monroe or James Dean," says Gregory. "But after their untimely deaths, there weren't hundreds of movies produced starring Marilyn or James Dean clones, nor are they exclusively associated with a genre. The men and women behind Bruceploitation built an international industry that was simultaneously epic and ephemeral, and its impact on global culture can still be felt today."

The Interviewees

BRUCE LE was born Huang Kin-lung in Burma (now Myanmar) in 1950. In 1974 he was discovered by a scout from Shaw Brothers when the studio needed a comic Bruce Lee-type for their TV and movie sitcom *Gossip Street*. Working as a contract player, Huang appeared in minor roles in Shaw productions like RIVALS OF KUNG FU (1974), BIG BROTHER CHENG (1975), and SUPER INFRAMAN (1975). When his contract expired, he made his first official Bruceploitation movie, THE BIG BOSS PART II (1976), in which he takes over the part that the real Bruce Lee played in the first film. He also met the Filipino Chinese director Joseph Kong (real name: Joseph Velasco) for their first of many Bruceploitation movies together, BRUCE'S FINGERS (1976). Now named Bruce Le, Huang worked with Velasco on eight additional Bruceploitation flicks, including BRUCE AND THE SHAOLIN BRONZEMEN (1980) and THE CLONES OF BRUCE LEE (1980). Le made at least twenty-five Bruceploitation movies between 1976 and 1982, most of them shot for P.T. Insantra, a smalltime Hong Kong company. Some of these were double sold in the U.S. and were playing in theaters under two different titles at the same time. Others were

re-edited with new footage and sent out again under new titles. Le later directed and starred in Bruceploitation films for producer Dick Randall – in one of these, BRUCE STRIKES BACK (1982), he co-stars with Randall's wife, Corliss, who's billed as 'Chick Norris' – and had a memorable cameo in Randall's Spanish-Italian gore film PIECES (1982). He remains active in the film industry to this day.

DRAGON LEE was born Moon Kyoung-seok in Korea in 1940. He trained in taekwondo with Kim Tai-Chung, who'd go on to double for Bruce Lee in GAME OF DEATH, and trained in hapkido with Hwang In-Shik, who plays a Japanese fighter that Bruce defeats during the climax of WAY OF THE DRAGON. Despite these connections, Moon found his way into the movie business when the guy who painted the billboards at his local cinema told him he looked like Bruce Lee and introduced him to Hwacheon Film Co. The studio immediately threw their new discovery into THE LAST FIST OF FURY (1977). Two of Hwacheon's Hong Kong partners, Tomas Tang and Joseph Lai, liked the idea of shooting Bruceploitation flicks on the cheap in Korea, so Moon was rechristened Dragon Lee and the pair quickly got to work. Together, they made over twenty Bruceploitation movies with Dragon Lee between 1977 and 1983, but they had a habit of recycling footage so it's hard to know the exact number. He's billed as Bruce Lei in WAYS OF KUNG FU (1978) among others, and Bruce Rhee on the U.S. posters and ads for KUNG FU FEVER (1979). Lee once owned a chain of movie theaters, still works in television, and is currently head of the South Korean equivalent of S.A.G.

A Taiwanese gymnast and physical education instructor who had taken some acting classes, Ho Tsun-Tao – alias **BRUCE LI** – was discovered by Taiwan's independent martial arts movie maestro, Joseph Kuo, who gave him small roles in some of his first movies before Ho landed the lead in the first Bruceploitation biopic, BRUCE LEE: SUPER DRAGON (1974). That movie and Ho's next Bruce biopic, BRUCE LEE: WE MISS YOU (U.S. title: THE DRAGON DIES HARD), were released in the States by Allied Artists, who got hit with lawsuits by Linda Lee for using her late husband's image in the ad campaigns for both movies. Charges of false advertising were also brought against GOODBYE BRUCE LEE: HIS LAST GAME OF DEATH (1975) by Pennsylvania's Consumer Protection Bureau after dozens of irate Lee fans who paid to see it at the Fox Theatre in Philadelphia complained that they were ripped off, leading a judge to file an injunction. Another biopic, BRUCE LEE: THE MAN, THE MYTH (1976), was so successful Stateside – especially in New York – that it's rumored to have been the reason for Barbra Streisand and Jon Peters aborting their own planned Bruce biopic (It was also the first English-dubbed Chinese kung fu movie to play on American television). Ho was offered the lead in GAME OF DEATH (1978) but turned it down when Golden Harvest refused to meet his careful conditions regarding the completion of Lee's unfinished film. Between 1974 and 1982, Ho Tsung-tao starred in some two dozen Bruceploitation movies, was the impersonator most respectful of Lee's legacy and the one least interested in being a celebrity. His last movie was PINK TRAP (1985). Today he is an accredited osteopath with his own clinic and teaches physical education to children and the elderly.

Siu-Lung Leung, better known as **BRUCE LEUNG** and **BRUCE LIANG**, was born Leung Choi-sang in Hong Kong in 1948. A former street brawler trained in Cantonese opera, Gōjū-ryū Karate and Wing Chun, he started off in the film business doing stunt work and supporting parts until a handful of lead roles in early Ng See-Yuen movies like CALL ME DRAGON (1974), LITTLE SUPERMAN (1974) and KUNG FU STING (1976) caught the attention of producers at the Goldig Film Company. They cast him as Bruce Lee in the infamous THE DRAGON LIVES AGAIN (1977). His

next films included BROKEN OATH (1977) with Angela Mao, the 3-D Jackie Chan movie MAGNIFICENT BODYGUARDS (1978) and appearing in and choreographing the action for THE TATTOO CONNECTION (1978) starring Jim Kelly. IRON FINGER (1978) with Bruce Li was a subsequent Bruceploitation entry, and SHOWDOWN AT THE EQUATOR (1978) and THE FISTS, THE KICKS AND THE EVIL (1979) were released in the U.S. as LEE LIVES WITHIN and LEE KICKS BACK, respectively. In the late '80s he disappeared from the film business but made a comeback a decade and a half later when Stephen Chow cast him as 'The Beast' in KUNG FU HUSTLE (2004). Leung would appear in almost 23 more films over the next few years.

DAVID CHIANG was born Chiang Wei-nien in Shanghai in 1947. His parents were movie stars and Chiang made his big-screen debut at age four. He landed at Shaw Brothers in his late teens but was mostly working there as a stuntman until director Chang Cheh took him under his wing, changed his name to David Chiang and paired him with another newcomer, Ti Lung, for a string of extremely popular martial arts movies beginning with HAVE SWORD, WILL TRAVEL in 1969. Both actors co-starred with Jimmy Wang Yu in RETURN OF THE ONE-ARMED SWORDSMAN, and when he departed Shaw Brothers the following year Chiang took over the role for THE NEW ONE-ARMED SWORDSMAN (1971), which was released in the U.S. as TRIPLE IRONS at the height of the kung fu craze. Two other Chiang movies that made a stateside splash that year were THE DUEL (U.S. title: DUEL OF THE IRON FIST) and THE WATER MARGIN (U.S. title: THE SEVEN BLOWS OF THE DRAGON). By that time, Chiang was moving into producing and directing while continuing to topline Shaw Brothers films including one of their U.K. co-productions with Hammer, THE LEGEND OF THE 7 GOLDEN VAMPIRES (1974). In addition to appearing in over 150 movies, he has directed fifteen features and is still acting in television shows and movies today.

A man of many pseudonyms, **GODFREY HO** was born either Ho Chi Keung or Ho Chi Keung in Hong Kong in 1948. He entered the film business through the Shaw Brothers as an assistant director to Chang Cheh on THE DEADLY DUO (1971), THE BOXER FROM SHANTUNG (1972), and THE SAVAGE 5 (1974) among others, and was also the AD on both of Shaw's co-productions with Hammer, THE LEGEND OF THE 7 GOLDEN VAMPIRES (1974) and SHATTER (1974). He made his official directorial debut in 1974 with PARIS KILLERS, which he co-directed with busy Shaw Brothers editor Ting-Hung Kuo. In the latter part of the '70s Ho went into partnership with producer Joseph Lai and formed Asso Asia Films for a string of kung fu movies featuring Dragon Lee, Hwang Jang-lee, Elton Chong, Casanova Wong and others. After 1982, many of his movies were made for Thomas Tang's Filmark Productions, starred American actor Richard Harrison, and had the word 'Ninja' in the title. No one seems to know exactly how many movies he's directed since he's used numerous pseudonyms and many consist of ninja footage spliced into unrelated films often shot years earlier, but the number is somewhere between 115 and 150. He retired from filmmaking over 20 years ago and was a teacher at the Hong Kong Film Academy.

SAMMO HUNG KAM-BO was born in Hong Kong in 1952, and at the age of nine joined the China Drama Academy where he and fellow students Jackie Chan and Yuen Biao were members of the Seven Little Fortunes, a Peking Opera theatrical and acrobatics troupe that trained under Sifu Yu Jim-yuen. The Fortunes appeared as extras in Hong Kong films and can be seen performing in the 1965 *I SPY* episode 'No Exchange on Damaged Merchandise'. Hung left the Academy in his teen years to pursue a career in the film industry, first at Shaw Brothers and then Golden Harvest, working as an actor, fight choreographer, stunt man and/or stunt

coordinator on myriad productions including *Enter the Dragon* (1973) and all of Angela Mao's star vehicles at GH. He was the first of the Fortunes to hit the big time when he started writing, producing, directing, and starring in his own films, beginning with THE IRON-FISTED MONK in 1977, and his ENCOUNTERS OF THE SPOOKY KIND (1980) kicked off a martial arts horror-comedy craze in Hong Kong. He founded or co-founded at least three different production companies, which turned out approximately one hundred and twenty-five movies between the late '70s and early '90s, including the MR. VAMPIRE, IN THE LINE OF DUTY, TIGER CAGE, POM POM and BLACK CAT series as well as standalone films starring Michelle Yeoh, Andy Lau, Brandon Lee and many others. In the '80s he reunited with his fellow Fortunes Chan and Biao together in PROJECT A (1983), WHEELS ON MEALS (1984), the LUCKY STARS trilogy (1983-1985), and DRAGONS FOREVER (1988), and individually on many other movies. His television series *MARTIAL LAW* ran for two seasons (1998-2000) on CBS and in one episode crossed over with Chuck Norris' *WALKER, TEXAS RANGER*. He's handled action director duties on films by Wong Kar-wai, Stephen Chow, Tsui Hark and many others, and is still working in motion pictures today after sixty-plus years in the business.

The prolific **PHILIP KO-FEI** was born Fai Ko Fei in Hong Kong in 1949. His movie career began at Shaw Brothers in 1971 as an actor-stuntman in several David Chiang-Ti Lung team-ups including DUEL OF FISTS (1971) and its sequel, THE ANGRY GUEST (1972). He played one of Mr. Han's many guards in ENTER THE DRAGON (1973) and came to the U.S. to throw punches and kicks in Al Adamson's blaxploitation/kung fu hybrid THE DYNAMITE BROTHERS (1974). In the latter half of the '70s he became stunt coordinator while continuing to act in numerous movies per year, alternating between good and bad guy roles and even starring in a few, including TWO WONDROUS TIGERS (1979), TIGER OVER WALL (1980), TWO ON THE ROAD (1980), and THE BOXERS OMEN (1983). In addition to appearing in over 200 movies with many of the top martial arts stars of the day, he directed over fifty features between his 1982 debut DIRTY ANGEL and his swan song twenty years later, KILLING SKILL (2002). Philip Ko-Fei succumbed to prostate cancer in March 2017, shortly after he was interviewed for ENTER THE CLONES OF BRUCE. He was 67.

Best known in the West for playing Bruce Lee's doomed sister in ENTER THE DRAGON (1973), Taiwan-born **ANGELA MAO YING** came from a family of Peking Opera entertainers, trained in ballet and Hapkido, and attended the Fu Sheng Peking Opera in Taipei. After graduation she moved to Hong Kong to look for work and was discovered by filmmaker Huang Feng, who got her a contract at the newly formed Golden Harvest movie studio. In May of 1973 her film DEEP THRUST (LADY WHIRLWIND) opened in New York City with full-page newspaper ads on the same day as Bruce Lee's FISTS OF FURY (THE BIG BOSS), and for a five-week period later that year she ruled American cinemas as three more of her movies – ENTER THE DRAGON, DEADLY CHINA DOLL and LADY KUNG FU – opened one after another. She appeared in eight movies with Carter Wong, four with Don Wong Tao, two apiece with Judy Lee and John Liu, worked for legendary director King Hu on THE FATE OF LEE KHAN (1973), trained in Taekwondo with Jhoon Rhee for WHEN TAEKWANDO STRIKES (1973), learned Muay Thai for THE TOURNAMENT (1974), shared top billing with James Bond one-timer George Lazenby in STONER (1974), became a big star in Japan (despite losing the lead role in SISTER STREET FIGHTER to Etsuko Shihomi), masterfully performed Jackie Chan's intricate choreography in the comical *Dance of Death* (1976), and co-starred with Tan Tao-liang in DUEL WITH THE DEVILS (1977), which ripped off Bruce Lee's concept for the unfinished GAME OF DEATH before Golden Harvest finished their version, and co-starred with Bruce Li in RETURN OF THE

TIGER (1978). Angela Mao Ying retired in the early '90s and moved to New York, where she owns several restaurants in the Bayside section of Queens.

Cheung Wing-Fat, better known under the screen name **MARS**, was born in 1954 and attended the Spring and Autumn Drama School, one of the top Peking opera schools and a rival of the China Drama Academy. Mars first stepped in front of the cameras as a child and teenager in several Shaw Brothers productions including King Hu's COME DRINK WITH ME (1966) and Chang Cheh's THE ONE-ARMED SWORDSMAN (1967). He met Jackie Chan at Golden Harvest when they were both performing stunts for the Bruce Lee movie FIST OF FURY (1972). In ENTER THE DRAGON (1973) Mars played the first of Mr. Han's incompetent guards to receive fatal punishment at the hands of Bolo Yeung, and soon after took a trip to Los Angeles to fight and perform stunts in Al Adamson's THE DYNAMITE BROTHERS (1974). His many collaborations with Jackie Chan and Sammo Hung stretch from the mid '70s to the early 2000's, and his experiences in the world of Bruceploitation movies include FIST OF UNICORN (1973), BRUCE LEE: THE MAN, THE MYTH (1976), Sammo's ENTER THE FAT DRAGON (1978), ENTER THREE DRAGONS (1978), GAME OF DEATH (1978), and GAME OF DEATH II (1980). Mars was last seen in the Benny Chan fantasy-comedy MONKEY KING (2020).

LO MENG was born Lo Quan Lam in Hong Kong in 1952. He studied martial arts for a decade and a half before his job as an accountant for Chang Cheh's production company led to supporting roles in a handful of the director's films for Shaw Brothers. His breakout role came in 1978 as the Toad (aka Number Five) in Cheh's popular THE FIVE DEADLY VENOMS, followed by several movies in which Cheh reused the same five or six lead actors (nicknamed "The Venoms" or "Venom Mob") including CRIPPLED AVENGERS (1978), INVINCIBLE SHAOLIN (1978), SHAOLIN RESCUERS (1979), THE DAREDEVILS (1979), THE MAGNIFICENT RUFFIANS (1979) and THE REBEL INTRUDERS (1980). Meng was the titular lead in THE KID WITH THE GOLDEN ARM (1979), the co-lead in TWO CHAMPIONS OF DEATH (1980) and ROAR OF THE LION (1981), and as a featured actor in several other Shaw Brothers productions until the studio closed in the mid '80s. He had a supporting role in John Woo's HARD BOILED (1992), but mostly worked in television before experiencing a big-screen comeback with IP MAN II (2008) and its two sequels, as well as Wong Kar-wai's THE GRANDMASTER (2013).

ANDRE MORGAN was a twenty-year-old American living in Hong Kong when he started working as an office boy at the Hong Kong movie studio Golden Harvest in June 1972. Because he could read and write Chinese, he was put in charge of English subtitling by the end of his first day. On his second day, he met Bruce Lee. Within a week, he was promoted to assistant manager in charge of sales, and a month later became an assistant producer on Lee's directorial debut, WAY OF THE DRAGON. For the next dozen years, Morgan was a CEO, partner and producer at the company, spearheading many international co-productions like THE MAN FROM HONG KONG (1975) and THE BOYS IN COMPANY C (1978), bringing Jackie Chan to the U.S. for his first English-language films in the early 1980s, and helping Tom Selleck with the transition from TV to film in HIGH ROAD TO CHINA (1983) and LASSITER (1984). He was one of the co-founders of the American Film Market in 1981, and that same year had a big hit with THE CANNONBALL RUN, one of his first collaborations with producer Albert S. Ruddy. The pair would go on to produce many movies and television series, including the CBS shows *WALKER, TEXAS RANGER* with Chuck Norris and *MARTIAL LAW* with Sammo Hung.

Born Chi-Wai Tsang in Hong Kong in 1953, **ERIC TSANG** got his start in the motion picture business as a stunt man and actor for the competing Shaw Brothers and Golden Harvest studios, working with the martial arts directors Chang Cheh, Huang Feng and Liu Chia-Liang. In 1977, the same year he played Popeye in the wacky Bruceploitation epic THE DRAGON LIVES AGAIN, Tsang had a minor role in Sammo Hung's directorial debut, THE IRON-FISTED MONK. He would go on to work with Hung many more times, most notably in the Bruceploitation comedy ENTER THE FAT DRAGON (1978), the LUCKY STARS series, MILLIONAIRE'S EXPRESS (1986), and PEDICAB DRIVER (1989). He's directed over twenty-five feature films including the first two hit comedies in the ACES GO PLACES series (1982 and '83, respectively) and the fourth in the LUCKY STARS series, LUCKY STARS GO PLACES (1986). In the U.S. he's best known for appearing in Wayne Wang's EAT A BOWL OF TEA (1989) and as Triad boss Hon Sam in the INFERNAL AFFAIRS trilogy. Tsang is currently the program director at Television Broadcasts Limited (TVB) of Hong Kong, where he hosted the popular variety show *SUPER TRIO STARS* for 18 years.

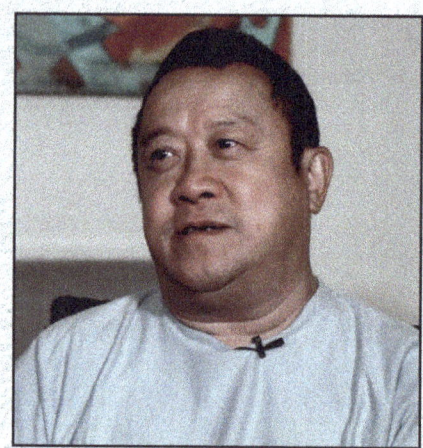

Martial arts movie director **LEE TSO-NAM** was born in Guizhou, China in 1943 and got his start in the business as an assistant director to Shan-Hsi Ting on THE GHOST HILL (1971) and the Jimmy Wang Yu classic FURIOUS SLAUGHTER (1972). One of his earliest directorial efforts, THE ESCAPER (1973), turned up in U.S. action theaters as 10 FINGERS OF DEATH to cash in on the Warner Brothers' hit 5 FINGERS OF DEATH. In the mid '70s he began a solid run of consistently entertaining movies, starting with a couple of Bruceploitation flicks starring Bruce Li – EXIT THE DRAGON, ENTER THE TIGER (1976), FIST OF FURY PART II (1977) and EDGE OF FURY (1978) – followed by THE HOT, THE COOL AND THE VICIOUS (1976), EAGLE'S CLAWS (1977), SHAOLIN INVINCIBLE STICKS (1978), Jim Kelly in THE TATTOO CONNECTION (1978), MISSION KISS AND KILL (1979), THE INVINCIBLE KUNG FU LEGS (U.S. title: THE INCREDIBLE DEATH KICK MASTER, 1980), the rape-revenge actioner THE WOMAN AVENGER (1980), and LADY PIRANHA (1982), aka LUNATIC FROG WOMEN starring Cheng Pei Pei. SHAOLIN VS. LAMA (1983) was a hit on 42nd Street and sampled by Wu Tang Clan ("Allow me to demonstrate the skill of Shaolin: the special technique of shadow boxing."). LIFE OF A NINJA (1983), CHALLENGE OF LADY NINJA (U.S. title: NEVER KISS A NINJA, 1984), KUNG FU WONDER CHILD (1986), and the 'girls with guns' favorite BEAUTY INVESTIGATOR (1992) are other worthwhile entries in his fascinating filmography.

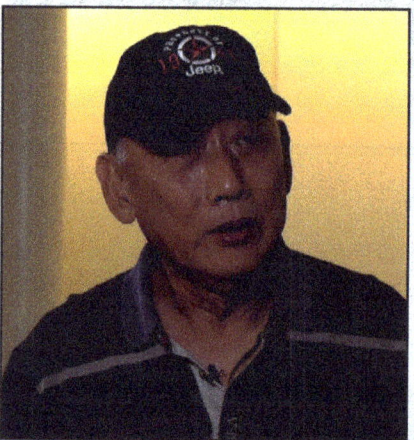

Born Kim Yong-ho in 1945, **CASANOVA WONG** was a Korean leg fighter who began appearing in movies the mid '70s when fancy kicking techniques were being popularized by Hwang Jang-lee, Tan Tao-liang, and John Liu. He appeared in a couple of movies in Korea, but his career took off when he went to Hong Kong and was discovered by Sammo Hung and director Feng Huang, who brought him to Golden Harvest for THE SHAOLIN PLOT (1976). A pair of movies directed by and starring Sammo, THE IRON-FISTED MONK (1977) and WARRIORS TWO (1978), came next. THE FEARLESS YOUNG BOXER (video title: METHOD MAN, 1979) and THE MASTER AVENGERS (1980) and were big influences on hip hop artists RZA and the Wu Tang Clan, and he continued to work through the 1980s, most notably in DUEL TO THE DEATH (1983). His Bruceploitation experiences include ENTER THE DEADLY DRAGON (1977), BRUCE AGAINST THE ODDS (aka LONE SHAOLIN AVENGER, 1978), BRUCE STRIKES BACK (1982), and appearing in GAME OF DEATH (1978) in a scene that was directed by Sammo for the Hong Kong cut, but also included in the international cut of GAME OF DEATH II (1980).

Born and raised in Brooklyn, **RON VAN CLIEF** – 'The Black Dragon' – joined the Marines and did boot camp in Camp Lejeune, where he claims an altercation on a bus led to a failed lynching that left him with twenty broken bones. He came back to New York and studied various martial arts styles with Moses Powell, Frank Ruiz, and Peter Urban before co-founding the Chinese Goju system with Owen Wat-son [sic]. He taught in open dojos around the city, and closed dojos in secret locations (one of them in the basement of the Empire State Building) where his students fought full contact. Producer-distributor Serafim Karalexis made him a movie star in THE BLACK DRAGON, which opened in Detroit in late 1974 and appeared on and off *Variety*'s list of 50 top grossers for the rest of the year, eventually earning over $6 million at the box-office. More films followed, including two of the Bruceploitation oddities THE DEATH OF BRUCE LEE (aka THE BLACK DRAGON'S REVENGE, 1975) and FIST OF FEAR, TOUCH OF DEATH (1980). Van Clief handled martial arts choreography on THE LAST DRAGON (1985), a Motown Pictures production starring one of his students, Taimak Guarriello, as a character nicknamed 'Bruce Leroy'. Van Clief also authored several books, including *The Manual of the Martial Arts* and *Black Heroes of the Martial Arts*, and produced the five-part instructional video/DVD *Chinese Goju*. In December 1994, at age 51, he took on Royce Gracie at UFC IV and retired from competition eight years later after winning the All-American Karate Championship. His autobiography, *The Hanged Man: The Story of Ron Van Clief*, was published in 2012.

YASUAKI KURATA, born in Japan in 1946, is a respected screen fighter who has appeared in dozens of films with everyone from Jackie Chan, Jet Li and Donnie Yen to Sonny Chiba, Jimmy Wang Yu and Chow Yun-fat. His father, an established master of Shitō-ryū Karate, owned a dojo and began instructing him at the age of eight. In his late teens, Kurata joined a movie studio trainee program but upon graduation failed to find steady work until some visiting Chinese producers offered him an acting gig. After co-starring in numerous Hong Kong and Taiwanese productions, including several from Shaw Brothers and First Films (and always playing villains), he returned to Japan to star in the TV series *FIGHT! DRAGON* and co-star with Sonny Chiba in THE EXECUTIONER (1974) and with Etsuko Shihomi in SISTER STREET FIGHTER: HANGING BY A THREAD (1974), RETURN OF THE SISTER STREET FIGHTER (1975), and DRAGON PRINCESS (1976) – all good guy roles. He was the heroic lead in WHICH IS STRONGER, KARATE OR TIGER? (1976), but when it showed up in U.S. theaters as THE TIGERS CLAW his name had been changed to Bruce Lo. For a re-release of KUNG FU, THE INVISIBLE FIST (1973), under the title THE REAL DRAGON, he was billed as Sonny Bruce. His other Bruceploitation experiences include getting beaten up by Bruce Leung in CALL ME DRAGON (1974), Bruce Li in EDGE OF FURY (1978), and Bruce Lee's buddy Unicorn Chan in FIST OF UNICORN (U.S. title: BRUCE LEE AND I, 1973).

LEE CHIU is known by many names including Chiu-Jun Lee, Chiao-Chun Li and Max Le Chiu-Chun. After background bits and walk-on parts in numerous Shaw Brothers productions such as VENGEANCE! (1970), THE SHADOW WHIP (1971) and MAN OF IRON (1972), his most memorable early role came in FIST OF FURY (aka CHINESE CONNECTION, 1972) as a student who is forced by Bruce Lee to eat a sign that has an anti-Chinese slogan written on it. He appeared with Richard Ng and Sammo Hung in the kung fu comedy WINNER TAKES ALL! (1977), the Hung-directed hit THE MAGNIFICENT BUTCHER (1979), and the two Ng See-yuen productions that launched Jackie Chan to stardom, SNAKE IN THE EAGLE'S SHADOW and DRUNKEN MASTER (both 1978), which led to him playing the Beggar So role in the Casanova Wong comedy THE MASTER STRIKES (1980). Working behind the scenes, he handled action choreography on CRAZY HORSE & INTELLIGENT MONKEY (1980), martial arts direction on

Joseph Kuo movies such as THE 36 DEADLY STYLES (1979), DRAGON'S CLAWS (1979), THE UNBEATEN 28 (1980) and SHAOLIN TEMPLE STRIKES BACK (1983), and made his directorial debut in 1984 with SHAOLIN VS. MANCHU. He also directed Kara Hui and Sibelle Hu in the action-horror hybrid WHO CARES (1989) and produced THAT'S MONEY (aka LETHAL ANGELS 2, 1990), starring Hui and Yukari Oshima/Cynthia Luster. He left the movie industry in the early '90s after producing the action film MOUNTAIN WARRIORS (1992), starring Waise Lee and Carrie Ng.

ROY HORAN was born in Laurel, Maryland in 1950. After college, he lived as a hunter/trapper among the First Peoples of the Northwest Territories for two years before moving to Japan, where he studied Gōjū-ryū Karate and got his black belt in Shorinji Kempo. During a trip to Taiwan he landed a part in a Bruce Lee biopic starring Ho Chung-tao (Bruce Li) called THE STORY OF THE DRAGON (1976), which became a hit and was released in the U.S. as BRUCE LEE'S SECRET, A DRAGON'S LIFE and BRUCE LEE'S DEADLY KUNG FU. He followed this with villain roles opposite John Liu in SNUFF BOTTLE CONNECTION (1977) and Jackie Chan in his breakout film, SNAKE IN THE EAGLE'S SHADOW (1978). The latter led to a job at writer-producer Ng See-yuen's Seasonal Films as the manager of international film sales and distribution. While there, Horan trained in Taekwondo with Hwang Jang-lee and later wrote, co-produced, and directed his groundbreaking feature-length instructional film, THE ART OF HIGH IMPACT KICKING (1981). Horan also made appearances in Seasonal's RING OF DEATH (1980), the Bruceploitation epic TOWER OF DEATH/GAME OF DEATH II (1981), the contemporary crime film GUN IS LAW (1983), and NO RETREAT, NO SURRENDER 2 (1987), which he also co-wrote. His daughter, born in 1985, is actress Celina Jade. After leaving the movie industry in 1991, Horan served as an adjunct professor at Hong Kong Polytechnic University and explored other interests related to science and education. His self-help book *Vigilance of the Heart* was published in 2018. He died on October 12, 2021 after hiking and meditating in the hills near Los Angeles. He was 71.

MIKE LEEDER left the UK for Hong Kong at age 21 and has since worked as a producer, consultant, and casting director on projects with some of the biggest names in the industry including Jackie Chan, Donnie Yen, Jean-Claude Van Damme, Jet Li, Tony Jaa, Iko Uwais, Scott Adkins and more. An acknowledged expert on action cinema, he has written for *Impact*, *Inside Kung Fu*, *Black Belt*, *Femme Fatales*, *Time Out*, *Budo* and *The South China Morning Post*, as well as creating Bonus Features and Audio Commentaries for more than 100 international DVDs and Blu-rays.

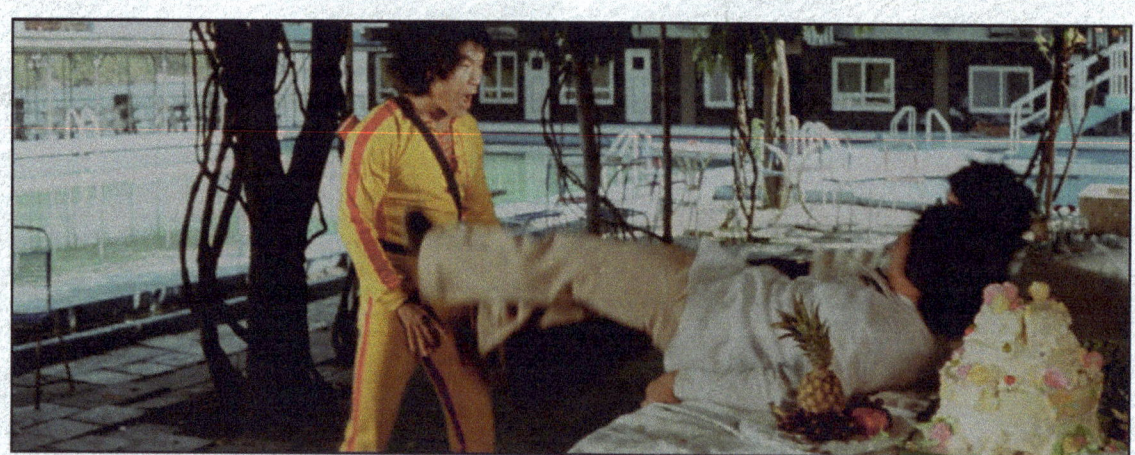

The Production Team

Executive Producer/Director David Gregory made his first feature-length documentary TEXAS CHAIN SAW MASSACRE – THE SHOCKING TRUTH in 2000 for the distribution company he co-founded, Blue Underground. He soon went on to direct – and often produce and edit – over 100 documentary features and shorts for DVDs that included THE DEER HUNTER, BADLANDS, FASTER PUSSYCAT! KILL! KILL!, HEATHERS and THE MAN WHO FELL TO EARTH, as well as the longer documentary projects THE JOE SPINELL STORY, BAN THE SADIST VIDEOS!, THE GODFATHERS OF MONDO and the IFC original production THE SPAGHETTI WEST. He made his narrative feature-directing debut in 2008 with PLAGUE TOWN, which he also co-wrote and co-edited.

Gregory co-produced and co-directed the 2011 Grand Guignol-inspired anthology horror feature THE THEATRE BIZARRE, and it was during post-production that David began the process of making LOST SOUL: THE DOOMED JOURNEY OF RICHARD STANLEY'S ISLAND OF DR. MOREAU. The documentary had its world premiere at London's Frightfest in August 2014 and its US premiere at Austin's Fantastic Fest a month later. It took the 'Best Documentary Award' at Sitges, the 'Director Award' at the Morbido Festival in Mexico, and collected additional awards at festivals in Melbourne, Sydney, and Cape Town. Gregory also served as co-producer on Stanley's return to feature directing after two decades, H.P. LOVECRAFT'S THE COLOR OUT OF SPACE.

Gregory's subsequent documentary feature BLOOD & FLESH: THE REEL LIFE & GHASTLY DEATH OF AL ADAMSON premiered at the Fantasia International Film Festival in July 2019. In 2020 he directed and co-produced TALES OF THE UNCANNY, a documentary on anthology horror featuring Roger Corman, Greg Nicotero, Tom Savini and over 50 more luminaries from the horror genre. TALES OF THE UNCANNY took the top award at Abattoir Festival in Wales where in premiered in October 2020.

In 2021, Gregory executive produced the landmark folk-horror documentary WOODLANDS DARK AND DAYS BEWITCHED. Hailed as "stunning" (*Diabolique Magazine*), "brilliant" (*AV Club*) and "mind-blowingly epic" (*Film

Threat), the film has screened at over 40 international festivals and received nearly a dozen major awards, including the Midnighters Audience Award at SXSW and Best Documentary at Fantasia International Film Festival.

David Gregory is co-founder and CEO of Severin Films, the production/distribution label dedicated to the world's most provocative cinema for physical media, theatrical, streaming and beyond. Founded in 2006, their distribution catalogue includes projects by iconic filmmakers Alejandro Jodorowsky, Roman Polanski, Dario Argento, Paul Morrissey, Mike Leigh, Lucio Fulci, Just Jaeckin, Peter Greenaway, Dennis Hopper, Joko Anwar, Patrice Leconte, Walerian Borowczyk, Sergio Martino, Álex de la Iglesia and UK comedy legends The Comic Strip. Severin has also elevated the oeuvres of such fringe auteurs as Andy Milligan, Al Adamson, Ray Dennis Steckler, Bruno Mattei, Frederick Friedel, Luigi Cozzi, Claudio Fragrasso, Umberto Lenzi, Juan Piquer Simón, Joe D'Amato and Goya-Award winner Jess Franco.

A veteran of the Hong Kong film industry for over 50 years, **Producer Jeremy Kai-Ping Cheung** began his career as a secretary for Sir Run Run Shaw at the legendary Shaw Brothers Studio in 1970 before getting promoted to supervising Southeast Asia distribution and post-production of all Shaw releases. He also assisted in distribution and marketing of Shaw films in Taiwan from 1977 to 1982. Jeremy founded My Way Film Company in 1987 and started acquiring films and TV series as well as investing in them. He has since produced over 200 films and continues to produce new films with stars such as Yuen Biao and Terry Fan as well as distributing films from Japan and Thailand for theatrical release in Hong Kong.

Producer Vivian Sau-Man Wong has close to 30 years experience in the Hong Kong and Asian entertainment media. She worked as acquisition manager for the Hong Kong office of Tai Seng Entertainment, the largest North American distributor of Hong Kong film and television content, from 1994 to 2012. She was content acquisition manager for Crunchyroll, the largest Video-on-demand subscription platform of Anime in North America. She's currently with Jungo TV, a streaming media company that provides entertainment content to both Southeast Asia and the Middle East.

A Hong Kong native who's known affectionately by Hong Kong Cinema fans worldwide as the 'Master of Remaster', **Producer Frank Djeng** was instrumental in bringing hundreds of classic Hong Kong action titles to North America in their original aspect ratio and with improved English subtitles when he was Marketing Manager for Tai Seng Entertainment from 1996 to 2008. He's been the co-host of the Kung Fu Superhero Extravaganza Panel at San Diego Comic Con since 1998, and he will be co-hosting there for the 26th time in 2023. He's widely considered to be one of the best audio commentators for Hong Kong cinema releases on Blu-Ray and 4K UHD, recording close to 50 commentaries a year for such prestige boutique labels as Severin, Arrow, Criterion, Eureka, 88 Films, Shout! Factory and Radiance Films.

Producer Michael Worth became obsessed as a 10-year-old with what was then known as 'Bruce Lee Rip-Off Movies'. His fascination with Kung Fu films led to a career as an actor and director of action and independent films – including the award-winning 2019 drama APPLE SEED – as well as the world's most formidable collection of Bruceploitation memorabilia. He is also author of the upcoming *You Must Be Tired of Living*, an exhaustive book project examining the sub-genre.

Director of Photography Jim Kunz is a filmmaker/cinematographer committed to preserving the genre films that might have been lost to time and decay, and is responsible for bonus features and restorations on hundreds of titles over the past two decades. He is best known for shooting and directing Elvira: Mistress of the Dark's recent *MOVIE MACABRE* television shows, as well as his work on the award-winning documentaries LOST SOUL: THE DOOMED JOURNEY OF RICHARD STANLEY'S ISLAND OF DR. MOREAU, BLOOD & FLESH: THE REEL LIFE & GHASTLY DEATH OF AL ADAMSON and THE FOUND FOOTAGE PHENOMENON. Jim is currently directing an upcoming documentary about the world of movie novelizations titled AND ALSO A MAJOR MOTION PICTURE.

Editor Douglas Buck first staked his claim as a genre filmmaker in the '90s with his shockingly violent short film critiques on American idealism and hypocrisy, which were eventually combined in the anthology feature film FAMILY PORTRAITS: A TRILOGY OF AMERICA for a 2003 theatrical run in both Paris and New York. Buck would eventually co-write and direct the 2007 Edward R. Pressman produced remake of Brian De Palma's cult classic SISTERS, starring Academy Award® nominees Chloe Sevigny and Stephen Rea. Along with his own directing career, Buck has edited over five feature length films for various auteur-minded directors, including David Gregory's LOST SOUL: THE DOOMED JOURNEY OF RICHARD STANLEY'S ISLAND OF DR. MOREAU.

About Severin Films

Severin Films is dedicated to the world's most provocative cinema for physical media, theatrical, streaming and beyond. Founded in 2006 by David Gregory, Carl Daft and John Cregan, Severin's curatorial and archival work has produced acclaimed collectors' editions and box sets – all with exclusive/extensive Special Features – that has placed the company at the forefront of the industry, while their original productions have won numerous awards on the international festival circuit.

Severin has produced the award-winning documentaries LOST SOUL: THE DOOMED JOURNEY OF RICHARD STANLEY'S ISLAND OF DR. MOREAU, BLOOD & FLESH: THE REAL LIFE & GHASTLY DEATH OF AL ADAMSON, and Kier-La Janisse's definitive exploration of folk horror, WOODLANDS DARK AND DAYS BEWITCHED, and co-produced original feature films that include PLAGUE TOWN and THE THEATRE BIZARRE.

The Severin distribution catalogue includes projects by iconic filmmakers Alejandro Jodorowsky, Roman Polanski, Dario Argento, Paul Morrissey, Mike Leigh, Lucio Fulci, Just Jaeckin, Peter Greenaway, Dennis Hopper, Joko Anwar, Patrice Leconte, Walerian Borowczyk, Sergio Martino, Alex de la Iglesia and UK comedy legends The Comic Strip; classics of Blaxploitation, Ozploitation and Nunsploitation; landmark American indies; groundbreaking horror from Spain, Turkey, France, Germany, Philippines, Canada, New Zealand, Poland, Indonesia and the Soviet Union, and the industry's most formidable collection of Italian gialli, cannibal, zombie, erotic thrillers and '80s action hits. Along the way, Severin has elevated the oeuvres of such fringe auteurs as Andy Milligan, Al Adamson, Ray Dennis Steckler, Bruno Mattei, Frederick Friedel, Luigi Cozzi, Claudio Fragrasso, Umberto Lenzi, Juan Piquer Simón, Joe D'Amato and Goya-Award winner – and Severin patron saint – Jess Franco.

The company's founders have long been outspoken champions of 'banned films'; Gregory and Daft's 2001 attempt to release an uncut edition of Wes Craven's LAST HOUSE ON THE LEFT in the UK led to a series of landmark legal appeals that became a global flashpoint for cinema's anti-censorship movement. Gregory's acclaimed 2005 documentary BAN THE SADIST VIDEOS! remains the definitive investigation of the 'Video Nasties' scandal and has led to Severin's restoration and release of more than 35 of the original 'condemned' titles.

Severin's webstore, monthly podcast, YouTube Channel, and annual Super-Shock Pop-Up Film Festival all continue to be popular genre fan destinations. Their subsidiary label Intervision is dedicated to eclectic '80s softcore favorites, shot-on-video oddities and regional rarities. And in 2019, the company launched the children's label Severin Kids to release such generation-scarring classics as THE PEANUT BUTTER SOLUTION and WHEN THE WIND BLOWS.

Severin has produced international projects for companies that include Second Sight UK, Kino Lorber, StudioCanal, Shout! Factory, Umbrella Entertainment, Arrow Video, MPI, The British Film Institute and The Criterion Collection.

THOMAS LEE INTERVIEW

By Simon Pritchard

SP: Do you remember when you were introduced to Bruce Lee?

TL: It was probably a poster, a VHS cover, or something like that. Growing up in the '80s it was almost impossible to not be aware of the guy.

SP: What was it like growing up just outside Boston?

TL: I was the only Asian kid in my class, so naturally, kids can be nasty, they made fun of me. For me, that was Bruce Lee. You know, I wrote the book and I think it's important that you know what racism does to your sense of identity and it makes you ashamed of things that you probably should be proud of. I have had a problematic relationship with Bruce Lee.

SP: How did you stay focused on your studies during that time?

TL: Yeah, especially being from Asian culture, you learn to blend in and try to keep to yourself. Put your head and work hard, you don't cause trouble. With my parents, that's 'family business' or don't talk about that stuff. I didn't get to do the things that most kids get to do. I didn't get to go to sleepovers, I didn't go camping, I didn't ride a bike. I think it's a combination of paranoia and the natural distrust of the outside world that immigrants tend to have. Whereas the more generations go forward, they are more open, they want to embrace America. But back then I had a good reason to be scared.

SP: How did you get into business journalism?

TL: It was in high school. I didn't think I was that great of a writer but I liked something about it. I always felt like an outsider looking in and I think that's actually a great mindset for journalists. I was there as an observer and watching, and that's what appealed to me. I would rather tell other people's stories rather than tell my own, although that changed over the years. I think it was a profession suited to my kind of mindset.

SP: You were awarded the Gerald M. Loeb Award for Distinguished Financial and Business Journalism, the highest honour in business journalism. How did that happen?

TL: I was a reporter at the Star Tribune in Minneapolis. There was a lot going on in retail at that time. A lot of transformation because of the internet. I broke some big stories and I think you create your own opportunities but you also seize you opportunities when they arise. So I too those stories and just made the most out o it. I won an award and wrote a book. I thin part of the mindset is that I feel like succes and opportunities are so fleeting, that yo should definitely make the most of them.

SP: And then COVID-19 happened, racism was becoming normalised again; Trump calling it the 'China virus'. What was it like for you and the Chinese community at this time?

TL: It was difficult. The trouble with the

Internet is the conspiracy theories that go out there and how people are easily led. I saw some old lady being attacked on the internet which actually happened in Oakland. I'm in Oakland right now talking to you. But it was also in New York / San Francisco and other places. It was especially old Chinese or Asian people that were attacked, this is really weird that they just come up and sucker punch them and run.

SP: I heard you spoke to your friend Janet Lee and discussed the Bruce exhibition. What made you want to join the project?

TL: I actually just lost my job and I guess I was a little depressed and anxious, but I called Janice just to catch up and she said, "Hey, we're doing this new exhibit on Bruce Lee". It was kind of cool because he was born in San Francisco Chinatown in 1940, and went to Hong Kong, but when he came back he didn't spend much time here; it was more the Oakland / Seattle way.

The interesting part is not many people know about Bruce's time in Oakland. That's where he really formulated his ideas for Jeet Kune Do. He opened up a martial arts school and really developed as a martial artist. But as I said, we were thinking of Bruce Lee and clearly has a connection with the Bay Area, but there's actually really nothing of his presence here. There are no statues, there's no street named after him. The only thing I could probably say is that the San Francisco Giants once released a Bruce Lee bobblehead.

We said, we have to honour Bruce and should do the museum exhibits. They had already spoken with Shannon Lee. I said I could volunteer and write some blogs or do some light writing, but I suddenly became a Tour Director and the Lead Curator. A part of the reason was that, as a journalist and as a storyteller, I was thinking there were new ways to apply storytelling to a different medium.

I welcomed it as I dove into the exhibit; rather than doing a Chronological thing, like people always do, you know, he was born in 1940. He did this in 1965, he did that, etc. We wanted to look at his life differently and there were several goals. Talking about COVID and how difficult it is to be Asian, but also a part of the goal was to highlight this really positive role model that everybody, white people, black people, Asian people used to love.

So we decided to look at his life and really exhibit it in a sort of a self-help way. Four

personas as a visionary, unifier, Shannon Lee and her book "Be Water" said Bruce Lee didn't want you to be Bruce Lee but he wanted to be the best possible version of yourself, so we have got to convey that message.

SP: Who supplied the materials and exhibits for the museum?

TL: Two collectors, Jeff and Perry, and Shannon Lee. We needed Shannon as she provided the standards and the depth we really needed. She provided us with items and I was going through them and I found the original letters and telefaxs between Ted Ashley and Bruce.

I think it is important that it's not what the letters say, but you have to put it in the right context to see what they are. Even when he's like, "OK, my career can't go along, I'll go to Hong Kong, he still kept in touch", he always felt like the goal was to come back to Hollywood.

Bruce shows resilience and tactics. He could have easily given up, but he always knew what his goal was. He kept in touch with Ted Ashley and whenever he had a blockbuster movie, he let Ted Ashley know about it. You know it's funny. It's casual, right? Bruce was very slick and now he's trying to work it in. He would say "Yeah my last movie did X amount and my valet is picking me up". Ted said things like "Congratulations on your success", and "I can't wait to work with you".

They even mentioned Enter the Dragon. They didn't say 'Enter the Dragon' but there was a dated telefax saying "I'm gonna begin work on this movie". I mean, it was the real deal.

One of the Collectors provided us with the original press materials from Hollywood. It was like a brochure. It talked about all the money that. It was kind of like a promotional brochure to try to pitch to theatres or distributors.

I talked to his friend, Doug Palmer, who said that Bruce asked him to look after his business affairs, Bruce may not have been particularly good with money, but he was Innovative, resilient, adaptive, and he had a vision. Bruce was organised with his brand, I mean Jeet Kune do, is not only a technical martial art, it's more of a philosophy, a way of thinking which is its own branding.

SP: What do you think about how Bruce branded himself?

TL: I quote Matthew Polly in the book; Bruce has two films, Way of the Dragon and Enter the Dragon, which has nothing to do with any plot in the movies. There's no one named the Dragon. It was like, Enter the Dragon. It was basically Bruce's coming out party. They wanted to call it Blood and Steel. He had to fight to have his name on it. OK, tell me what movie star today has a movie named after themselves?

I would say that I used that in the book

as the prime example of his approach to innovation. So we go back to him going to Hong Kong, the Shaw Brothers, and all those Kung Fu movies, there was great escapism, especially for those living in the stress of Hong Kong. But when you watch them, it's just like endless fighting. You know, it's great to watch, but Bruce Lee wanted to elevate that genre, so what he did was, a part of his approach to innovation was very much like Steve Jobs, To be innovative, you don't need to create something out of anything, You take existing things to combine them together and whatever, and it that the result is the product gets better.

So he took the exciting kinetic action of those Hong Kong movies, and combined it with the character story-driven approach of Hollywood and the result was a movie, well, imperfect but it elevated and transcended the martial arts genre. Bruce focused on the motivations of his character, the revenge for his sister for example, and the idea of fighting itself was important.

It's all about the personalisation, Bruce puts

Eastern Heroes: Bruce Lee Special Vol.2 #3

his stamp on the movie. In the beginning

In Enter the Dragon there was one scene I focused on in the book which was when he fought O'Hara, the guy that killed his sister. When I was talking to Shannon about it, it was such a great scene because it showed his approach to violence. It was a violent guy who was killed,

SP: As a business journalist, how has Bruce influenced the way you approach your work?

TL: It's about recognising opportunity and seizing it. I probably would have been fine just being a journalist, but what? I took what happened, as a journalist and made it into books. The museum exhibits, you see, it's you meeting people, it's you. I think Bruce Lee would have mostly approved of that.

I talk in the book about how Bruce deliberately cast a wide net in the socio-economic circle, he had his friends and colleagues, but he was curious. That's a big part of what he's about. He was writing ideas down, he was reading. Bruce was sending correspondence and was trying to come up with an idea for a television show in America about women's self-defence. I'm like, what the fuck right? That would have been groundbreaking, so it could be groundbreaking. He also wrote poems to cheer up his friends back home. Those letters are out there somewhere.

SP: One interesting point you make in your book is that everyone now loves Enter the Dragon and it's the greatest martial arts film ever, but this was just the start of his time at Warner Brothers. Bruce would have progressed, what direction do you think Bruce would have gone?

TL: I think it was pretty obvious it would have been changed to direct and write movies. He would have still had his production company, who knows? Maybe he would have been the head of the studio.

There is no doubt he would have a five-picture deal with Amazon Prime or Netflix. It would be huge in streaming, Bruce would have been huge on social media. Bruce would have transcended more businesses as he actually designed clothes and jewellery, possibly fashion.

The real question is whether he would have embraced his role as an iconic Asian American in the political and social sense. You look at him as an icon because of what he did, but he didn't go out there preaching about racial or voting rights, he didn't march. He does believe in living by example. He was also smart because he knew he was gonna be Hollywood. So would he have been more vocal in terms of being a leader of the Asian American community now? And so I think that he would have had the money, the tools, the platform it's almost like the Sky's the limit of what he could have achieved. As an actor, I would hope he would have transcended the martial arts genre because a lot of successful Asian American people are doing martial arts. There's nothing wrong with that. That's how they get to success but Bruce has done this. Could he headline a romantic comedy? could Bruce have done Shakespeare or a prestige drama? I think of Bruce as someone who perfected his craft but was only at the beginning. That's what is so tragic as it would have been great to see him fully grow.

SP: What's your favourite Bruce Lee film?

Oh, it's Enter the Dragon. The cross-over of the international cast, the elevation of the hero, the lot.

SP: What's the feedback you've got personally from the book?

TL: People would say, "Oh, I never thought about it like that" or "You took different parts of it

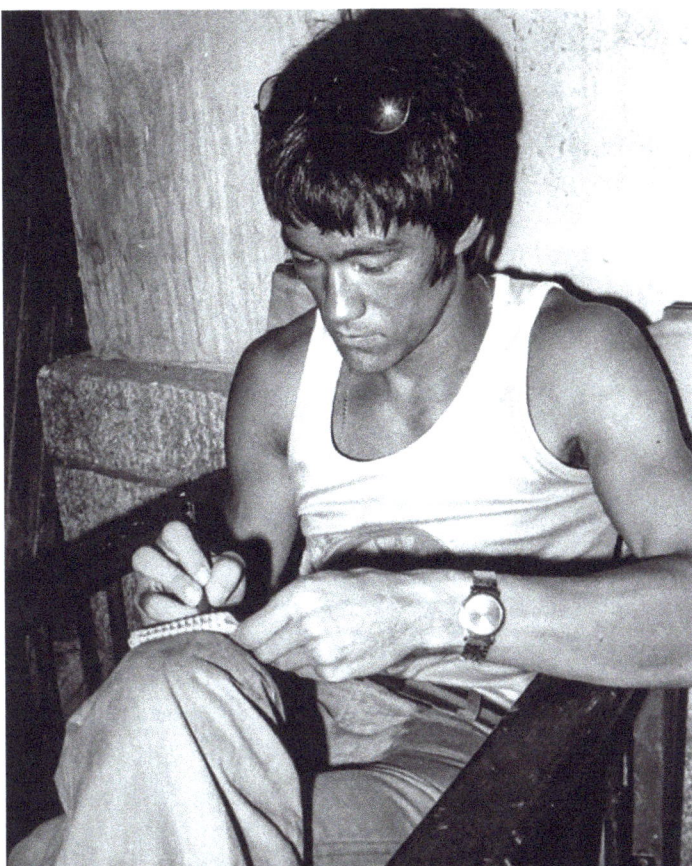

I knew, and you put it together." In the beginning of the book I talk about myself and there are people that really relate to that. People ask me realised that I have been doing it, taking a huge opportunity and bringing something into existence. Yeah hanging out with a lot of people, the actual collaboration itself.

SP: Is this a one-off book for you? Do you think there's more behind this now?

TL: I am personally satisfied with it as it is. But I think Natasha said they were interested in a series of books. I don't know where we stand with that, but one thing that was kind of cool about the Bruce Lee code is that it's being published in other parts of the world now. I think I accomplished what I wanted to do which was to provide a unique interpretation of Bruce's Life.

SP: Thank you for speaking with us and speak soon.

FIST OF FURY
NIGHT OF THE DRAGON

#2 2023

This issue we get a look inside the latest offering from Mike Kelly
Complete with excellent cover artwork By Steve Morris
Available for commissioned work
https://www.facebook.com/steven.morrisartist
Now available to order:
https://www.kungfu-comics.com/?fbclid=IwAR062bBJvVnsnve2XgpKuYxmOCAlYjATS_upuPfTwf6ZXs1kxqH96e_X4CY

Eastern Heroes: Bruce Lee Special Vol.2 #3

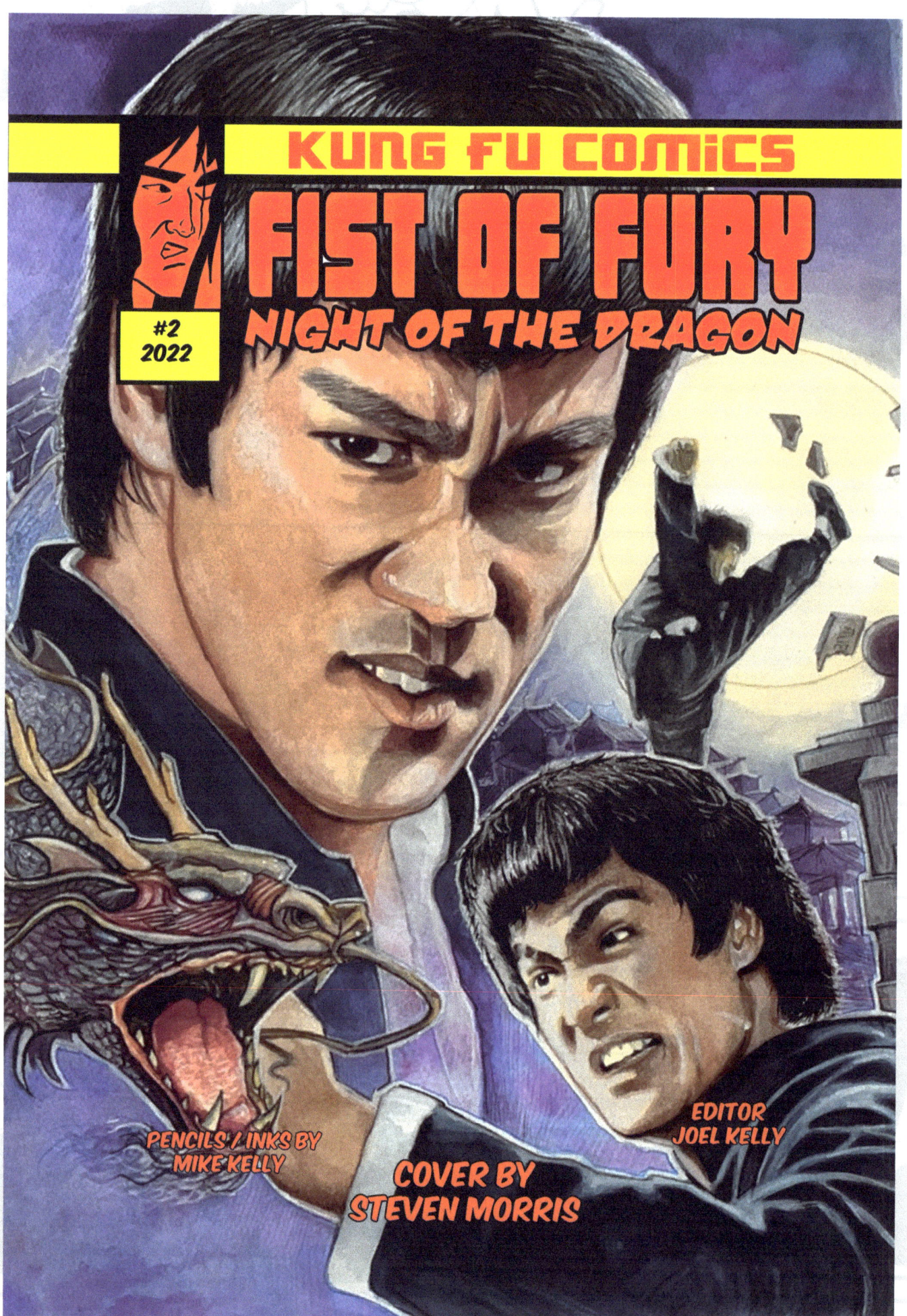

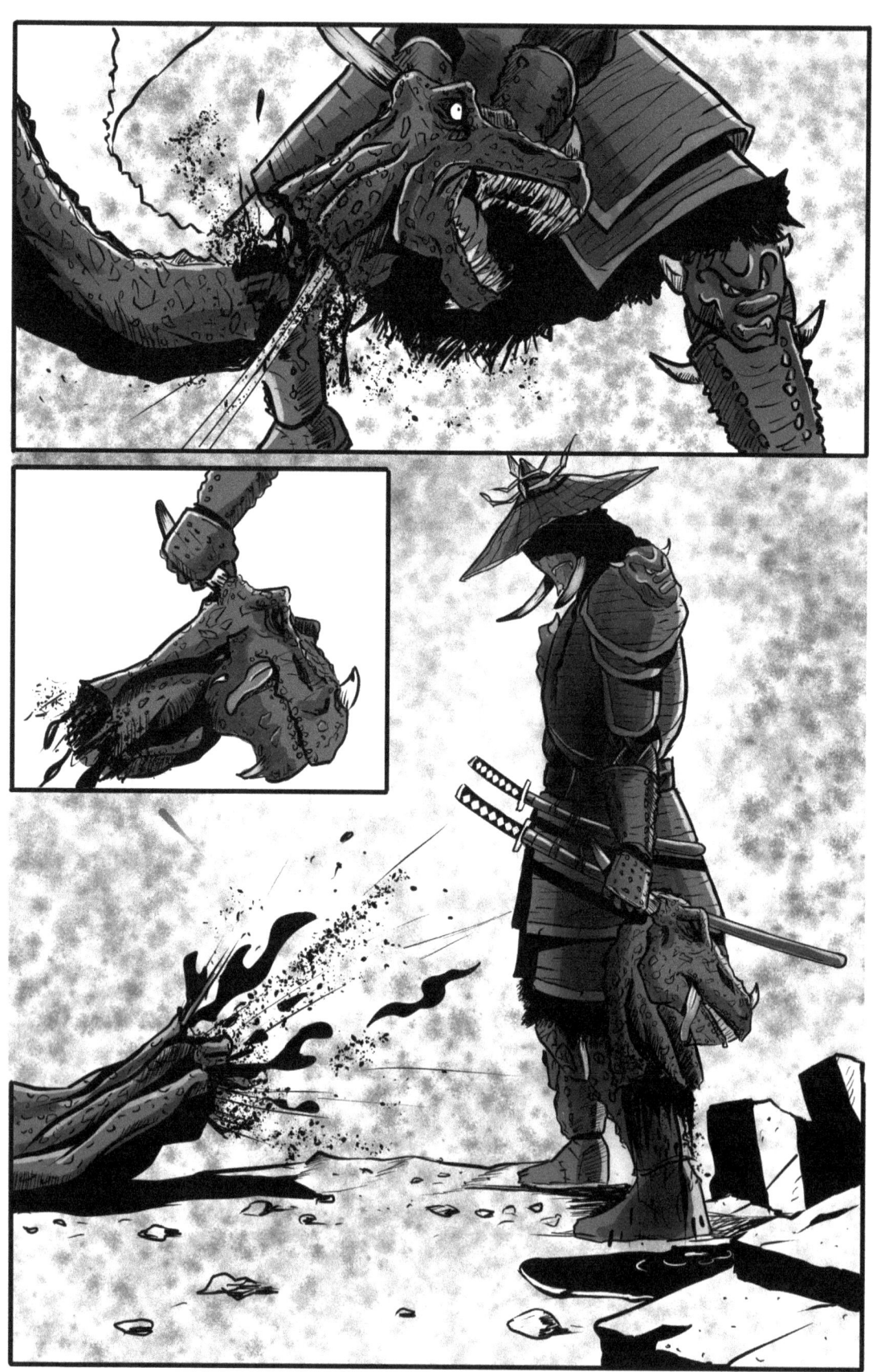

THE ROOFTOP GALLERY

Eastern Heroes: Bruce Lee Special Vol.2 #3

Eastern Heroes: Bruce Lee Special Vol.2 #3

By Johnny Burnett

Greetings once more Dear Friends! 2023 is seeing a wealth of new Bruce Lee releases onto Physical Media and following on from Arrow Video's incredible Bruce Lee at Golden Harvest Boxset (which i covered at length in the previous Enter The Dragon special issue) Arrow are following up on the success of their boxset by listening to those who called for individual releases of Bruce's movies and giving us just that, stand-alone releases of all four of Bruce's HK movies onto Bluray and 4K UHD versions…

A release date of November 13th has been confirmed just as we went to print, let's take a quick look at what Arrow have put together for the The Big Boss, Way of The Dragon, Fist of Fury and Game of Death!

(As with the boxset, these are all UK only releases as Criterion still hold the rights for the movies in the US of A…)

The Big Boss

Available in Bluray and 4K UHD version
Region B Locked - UK release Only.
ETA - 13th November 2023

This essentially gives us the exact same on disc extras as the two Big Boss Discs in the Boxset, but without the printed extras which came with that boxset. The full spec for the 4K release are as follows, the Bluray release has all the same extras, but in standard 1080p - the main draw here for most will be the longer Mandarin Cut of the movie, no Saw in the head scene yet, it remains lost to time...

DISC 1: The Big Boss

• 4K (2160p) Ultra HD Blu-ray presentation in Dolby Vision (HDR10 compatible) of the 99-minute 1983 version of The Big Boss, restored by Arrow Films from the original negative
• Original restored Mandarin, English and Cantonese mono audio
• Two English mono options, the standard mix and a Japanese mix with alternate score
• English subtitles, plus optional subtitles for the deaf and hard-of-hearing for the English dubs
• Two feature commentaries, one by David Desser and one by Brandon Bentley
• Two alternate versions with lossless mono audio: the English Export Cut, featuring a rare alternate English dub track (some scenes in Mandarin); and the 100-min US Theatrical Cut
• Return to Thailand, a documentary produced and presented by Matt Routledge exploring the original filming locations
• Recently uncovered deleted and extended scenes, with optional commentary by Bentley

• The Not-Quite-Biggest Boss, a video essay by Bentley investigating the scenes still lost, such as the 'saw-in-the-head' scene
• Archive interviews with co-star Lau Wing and stuntman Tung Wai
• Bruce Lee Vs. Peter Thomas, a short video essay about the music for the English version
• Alternate credits sequences
• Trailer gallery, including a 'Before The Big Boss' reel and the trailer for lost sequel The Big Boss Part II
• Image gallery

DISC 2: The Big Boss - the Mandarin Cut

• 4K (2160p) UHD Blu-ray presentation in Dolby Vision (HDR10 compatible) of the 110-min Mandarin Cut of The Big Boss, restored by Arrow Films
• Original lossless mono audio
• English subtitles for the Mandarin Cut
• Axis of English, a video essay by Will Offutt profiling the English dubbing actors for The Big Boss, Fist of Fury and The Way of the Dragon
• Unrestored raw scan of the Mandarin Cut (1080p only)
• Illustrated collector's booklet featuring writing on the film by Walter Chaw
• Reversible sleeve featuring original and newly commissioned artwork by Tony Stella

Fist of Fury

Available in Bluray and 4K UHD versions
Region B Locked - UK release Only.
ETA - 13th November 2023

My own personal favourite of Bruce's HK films, and again we see Arrow porting over all the on-disc extras from the Boxset, for those that may have missed the breakdown of the boxset previously, it's a fairly loaded set, on the 4K UHD release we get:

• 4K (2160p) UHD Blu-ray presentation in Dolby Vision (HDR10 compatible),

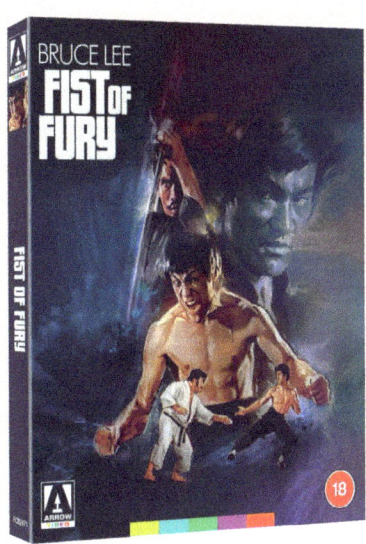

restored by Arrow Films from the original negative
• Alternate 'English Export Cut' viewing option with different opening and closing credits via seamless branching and alternate lossless mono audio
• Original restored Mandarin, English and Cantonese mono audio
• English subtitles, plus optional subtitles for the deaf and hard of-hearing on the English dubs
• Two feature commentaries, one by Jonathan Clements and one by Brandon Bentley
• Legend of the Dragon, an 82-minute overview of Lee's life and career by film critic and historian Tony Rayns
• Visions of Fury, a featurette on Bruce Lee's collaboration with Golden Harvest and Lo Wei, featuring interviews with co-producer Andre Morgan and martial arts experts Michael Worth, Frank Djeng, John Kreng, Andy Cheng and Bruce Willow
• New Fist Part Two Fist, a video essay by Bentley looking at the two competing sequels shot simultaneously in 1976
• Archive interviews with co-stars Nora Miao, Riki Hashimoto, Jun Katsumara and Yuen Wah

Alternate credits sequence
• Trailer gallery, including a Chen Zhen trailer reel
• Image gallery
• Illustrated collector's booklet featuring writing on the film by Walter Chaw
• Reversible sleeve featuring original and newly commissioned artwork by Tony Stella

Again, the regular Bluray version, includes all the same extras…

Way of the Dragon
Available in Bluray and 4K UHD versions
Region B Locked - UK release Only.
ETA - 13th November 2023

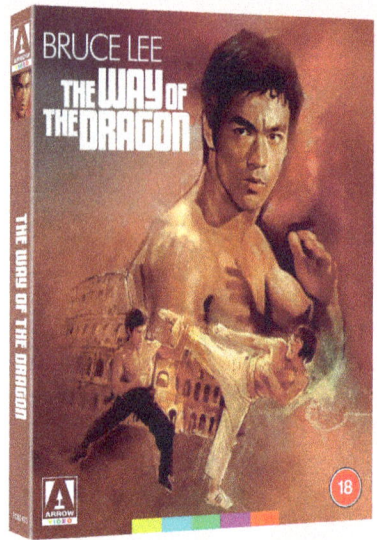

The standout extra for me on the Arrow Bruce lee at Golden Harvest boxset, was the mammoth, The Final Game of Death video essay, Arrow has opted to include this on the standalone release of Way Of The Dragon, likely as WOTD remains Bruce's only completed movie as Director, and his original concept for Game of Death (which the Final Game of Death essay celebrates and explores in depth) sits alongside Way of The Dragon far more effectively than it does alongside Robert Clause's Game Of Death feature film.

DISC 1: The Way of The Dragon
• 4K (2160p) UHD Blu-ray presentations in Dolby Vision (HDR10 compatible), restored by Arrow Films from original film elements, of the Hong Kong Theatrical Cut and the Japanese Cut via seamless branching

• Original newly restored lossless Mandarin, English and Cantonese mono audio on the Hong Kong Theatrical Cut
• Alternate lossless English mono audio on the Japanese Cut
• Optional English subtitles
• English subtitles for the deaf and hard-of-hearing on both English audio options
• Two feature commentaries, one by Frank Djeng & Michael Worth and one by Brandon Bentley
• The Way of the Camera, a documentary looking at Lee's filmmaking and fighting method in his directorial debut, featuring interviews with Golden Harvest producer Andre Morgan, martial arts experts Michael Worth, Jon Kreng, Andy Cheng, Frank Djeng, David Yeung, film historian Courtney Joyner and actors Piet (Peter) Schweer, Jon Benn and John Saxon
• Meet the Italian Beauty, a newly filmed interview with star Malisa Longo

• The Scottish Soldier Meets the Dragon, a newly filmed interview with on-set observer John Young
• Newly recorded select scene commentary by 'thug' actor Piet Schweer
• Archive interviews with co-stars Jon Benn, Bob Wall and Hwang In-shik and production managers Chaplin Chang and Louis Sit
• Trailer gallery, including a Bruceploitation trailer reel
• Image gallery
• Illustrated collector's booklet featuring writing on the film by Walter Chaw
• Reversible sleeve featuring original and newly commissioned artwork by Tony Stella

DISC 2: The Final Game of Death (BLU-RAY)
• The Final Game of Death, a brand new 223-minute video essay by Arrow Films that incorporates a new 2K restoration of all two hours of Lee's original dailies from a recently-discovered interpositive
• English subtitles for the deaf and hard-of-hearing
• Game of Death: Revisited, an earlier attempt to reconstruct Lee's original vision from 2001
• Super 8 footage from 1974 of Dan Inosanto demonstrating the nunchaku
• Brief archival interview with Kareem Abdul-Jabbar from 1976
• Image gallery

Game of Death
Available in Bluray and 4K UHD Versions
Region B Locked - UK release Only.
ETA - 13th November 2023

The standalone release for Game of Death also gives us Game Of Death 2 and the HK version of the movie Tower Of Death, a far more fitting counterpart for the Clause feature film.

DISC 1: Game of Death (4K UHD or Bluray depending on the version purchased)
• 4K (2160p) UHD Blu-ray presentation in Dolby Vision (HDR10 compatible), restored by Arrow Films from original film elements, of the international cut and the Japanese cut of Game of Death via seamless branching
• Brand new 2K restoration of the International Cut of Game of Death II by Arrow Films from original film elements
• Original restored English mono audio on both cuts
• English subtitles for the deaf and hard-of-hearing
• Feature commentary by Brandon Bentley & Mike Leeder
• The Song I'm Singing Tomorrow, an interview with star Colleen Camp
• Deleted and extended scenes from the Chinese-language versions of the film, including two alternate endings (some material in standard-definition)
• Archive interviews with co-stars Dan Inosanto and Bob Wall
• Behind-the-scenes footage as featured in Bruce Lee: The Legend
• Rare pre-production sales featurette from 1976 with new commentary by Michael Worth and producer Andre Morgan
• Fight scene dailies directed by Sammo Hung
• Locations featurette from 2013
• Trailer gallery, including Bruceploitation and 'Robert Clouse at Golden Harvest' trailer reels
• Image gallery

DISC 2: Game of Death II / Tower of Death (BLU-RAY)
• High Definition (1080p) Blu-ray presentation of Game of Death II as well

is the Hong Kong Theatrical Cut titled Tower of Death (contains some standard-definition material)
• Original lossless English mono audio on Game of Death II
• Original lossless Cantonese, Mandarin and English mono audio on Tower of Death
• English subtitles for the deaf and hard-of-hearing on Game of Death, and optional English subtitles on Tower of Death
• Feature commentary by Frank Djeng & Michael Worth, co-producers of Enter the Clones of Bruce Lee
• Archive interview with co-star Roy Horan
• Alternate Korean version with unique footage, presented in High Definition with original lossless mono audio and English subtitles

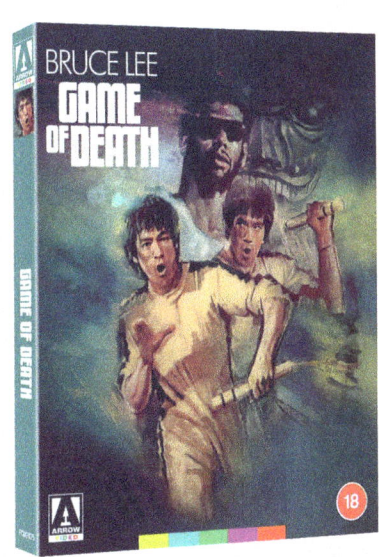

• Alternate US video version in High Definition with lossless English mono audio, via seamless branching
• Alternate end credits sequence for Game of Death II
• Trailer gallery
• Image gallery

So for all of you who passed on the boxset, or for the die hard gotta buy it all Bruce Lee collectors out there (of which there are a great many!) Then these sets will be a welcome addition to your collections when they hit the shelves later this year!

In other news, Warner Brothers also put out two somewhat lacklustre releases of two Jackie Chan movies as HMV exclusives, both of these are already available in store and on HMV's website, and as with the Bruce Lee releases, these are both UK only releases…

Rumble in the Bronx
HMV Cine Edition
Bluray

All hopes of us finally getting a decent release of the HK cut of the movie were dashed upon release as this is once again the Miramax or US release of the movie, all of Warner brothers minimal efforts seem to have gone into producing a few printed materials.
You get a A3 poster, 3 double sided art cards (which to add insult to injury appear to be reproductions of the HK lobby cards) and a pretty useless 'anatomy of an action hero- art card.
For those who don't yet own the movie or for those looking to upgrade from DVD, the set will be a welcome upgrade. but it's very much a missed opportunity in my eyes..

Drunken Master 2
HMV Cine Edition
Bluray

Similar story here with DM2, whilst we are getting the international version of the movie (thankfully not the dreaded Miramax Legend of Drunken Master edit) this is the same remaster that Warner's put out a year or so ago in the US with a few new printed extras, namely a double sided A3 poster, 12 page booklet and 3 double sided artcards.
I would still recommend the Japanese release of the movie, which is uncut and a far better presentation overall. You can check out a video breakdown of that Japanese edition over on my youtube channel along with loads of interviews, unboxings and reviews!

That's it for this issue, thanks for reading!

www.youtube.com/thefanaticaldragon

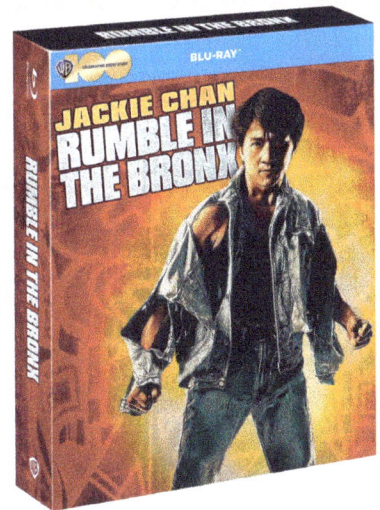

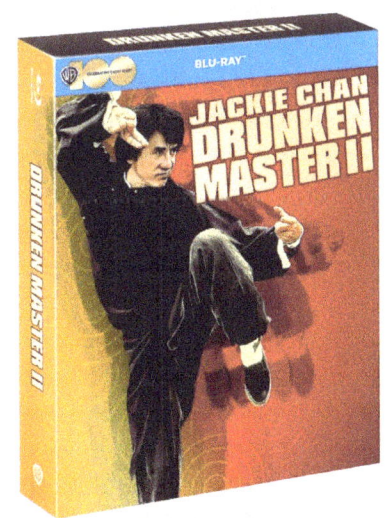

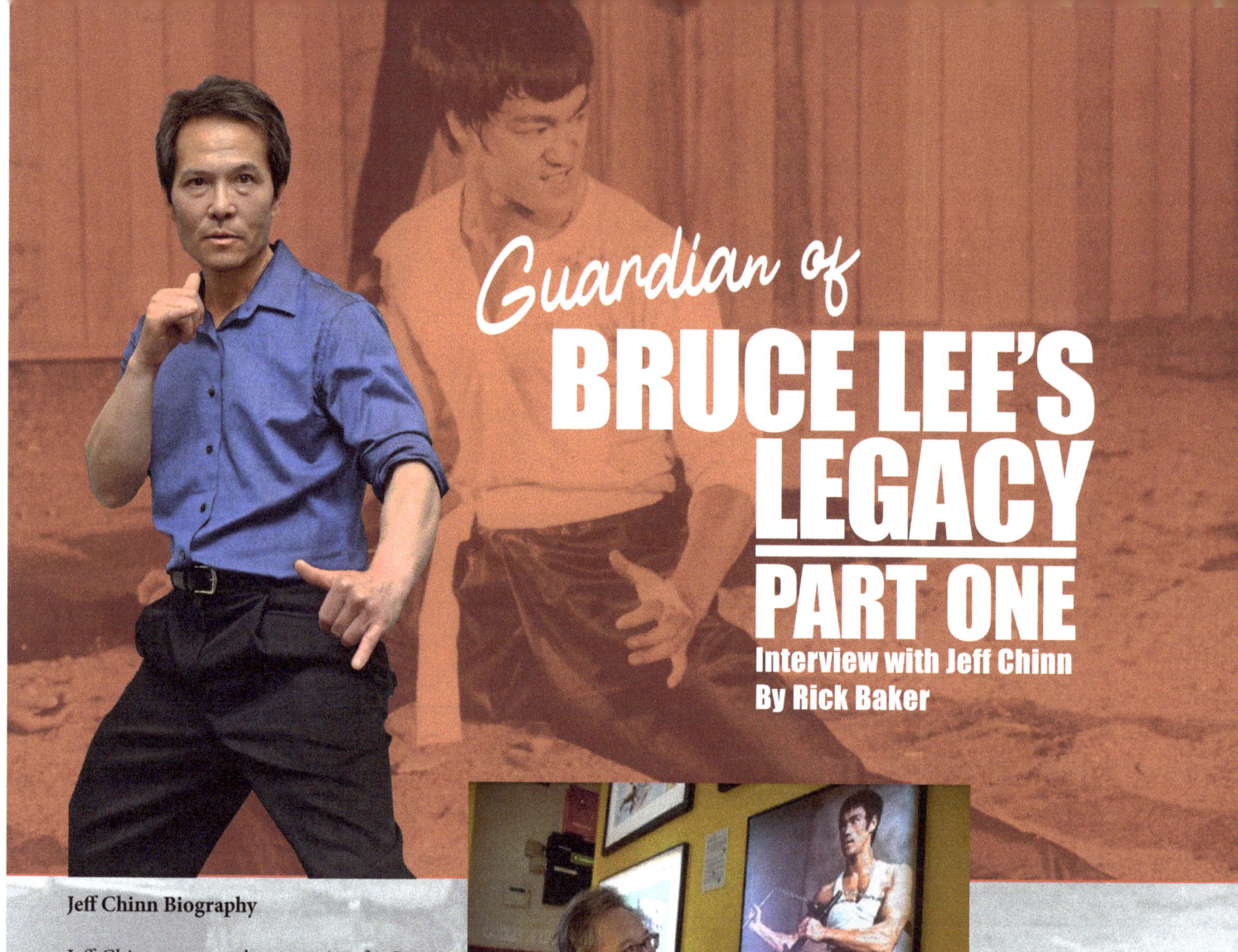

Guardian of BRUCE LEE'S LEGACY
PART ONE
Interview with Jeff Chinn
By Rick Baker

Jeff Chinn Biography

Jeff Chinn, a man whose passion for Bruce Lee has transformed him into a renowned collector of Bruce Lee memorabilia. While his collection may seem larger than life, Jeff's true essence is remarkably down-to-earth. At 61 years old, he's a retired postal worker with the appearance of a handsome Southern Chinese uncle, exuding the vitality of a lifelong athlete.

When you think of collectors, you might envision meticulously preserved comic books, action figures displayed in glass cases, rows of pristine sneakers, and binders filled with colourful Pokémon cards. Collectors are known for their meticulous nature, unwavering passion, and their penchant for guarding their treasures with secrecy. Many collectors prefer to interact exclusively with their peers, seeking out the rarest items as if they were adding elusive dragons to their treasure hoard. Jeff Chinn, much like his counterparts, possesses a deep commitment to organization and attention to detail. Yet, he stands out for his willingness to share his remarkable collection with others. The dedicated "Bruce Lee room" in his home has hosted hundreds of visitors, and he has generously lent his most prized possessions to museums for over two decades. His motivation transcends mere financial gain; it is instead a quest to spread Bruce Lee's legacy of self-love and pride to future generations of Asians across the globe.

The journey that led Jeff Chinn to embrace this mission is both poignant and inspiring. In his childhood, he endured relentless bullying that took a toll on his health, resulting in a stomach ulcer. One fateful day, with tears in his eyes, he looked at the Bruce Lee poster on his bedroom wall and implored the martial arts icon to help him through his ordeal. In return, Jeff made a solemn promise to Bruce Lee, a commitment that has guided his life's purpose ever since.

Guardian of Bruce Lee's Legacy interview

Rick: Hi Jeff, nice to meet you and thanks for taking the time out for this interview

Jeff: Nice to meet you too Rick

Ricky: Anyway, even though we've never met in person, I've known about you for quite some time. I wanted to start by delving into your Bruce Lee enthusiasm. Did it begin around 1973, or were you a fan even before that, possibly through your exposure to the Green Hornet?

Jeff: What somewhat frustrates me is that there are some significant Bruce Lee collectors who claim they became fans by watching the Green Hornet. To be honest, some of those individuals, some of those fans, were so young back then that they were more likely fans of Kato, not Bruce Lee. I could easily say that I also began in 1966 when the Green Hornet aired, but I can truthfully admit that I wasn't a Bruce Lee fan at that time. I was a fan of Kato.

Rick: In the UK, we got the Green Hornet series later. So for any UK folks who say they were Green Hornet fans were more likely to have been Kato fans as well.

Jeff: what took so long?

Rick: You know, I think the delay might have been due to the immense popularity of the Batman series. They probably assumed "the Green Hornet" would have the same success and Bruce as kato had captivated by Bruce Lee's martial arts skills or his charisma, at least not until his later movies or "Longstreet." So, did you watch it as a young person before you got into Bruce Lee's films?

Jeff: Yes, it was in 1966, and I was around five years old.

Rick: Same here, we're about the same age. What was your introduction to Bruce Lee like?

Jeff: My introduction to martial arts or Kung Fu on TV was through Kato in the Green my friend told me to ask my dad to take me to a Bruce Lee movie. At that point, I wasn't a Bruce Lee fan. The magazine had a picture of Bruce Lee with Unicorn Chan, and I asked a silly question: "Which one is Bruce Lee?" My friend clarified that it was the guy giving a thumbs-up without a shirt. Bruce Lee's appearance had changed from his Green Hornet days to his Kung Fu movie days, which led to this picture becoming my first Bruce Lee item in my collection. I showed it to my dad and asked if we could see a Bruce Lee movie. He hesitated and said, "Where?" I suggested Chinatown, but he refused due to the dirty condition of the Chinese theatres. I

made a couple of appearances in the "Batman", but, you know, I think you and I are on the same page here. People have tried to convince me otherwise, but I've watched the Green Hornet many times, and Bruce Lee never really stood out to me, at least not in the way he did in later works like "Longstreet." It's challenging for me to understand. I do feel like some collectors enjoy trying to one-up each other by saying, "Yeah, I was into this way back in '66," and I'm not saying they didn't like the Green Hornet or Kato, but, as you mentioned, I don't think they were Hornet. Growing up in San Francisco, we had numerous Chinese movie theatres, and they had speakers in front of the theatre so you could hear the fighting sounds while passing by. That piqued my interest. However, my dad never took me to see these movies. I got interested in Kung Fu films by seeing the posters and lobby cards in front of these theatres. It wasn't until February 1972, during ABC's Tuesday Movie of the Week, that I saw the pilot for Kung Fu. This was my first Kung Fu movie. Around the same time, a friend gave me a Hong Kong magazine called New Martial Hero. At the end of 1972, even offered to lift my legs off the ground to avoid mice, but he still said no. It wasn't until March 1973, when Warner Brothers released "Five Fingers of Death," that I asked my dad again. This time, he agreed because it was in a clean downtown theatre. This marked the beginning of my journey into the Kung Fu craze, leading to the discovery of Bruce Lee and his film "The Big Boss."

Rick: I was similar to you. I was 14 when "Enter the Dragon" was released, and I had developed a fascination because of a small newspaper clipping showing Bruce

school kids to get in. I watched "The Big Boss" along with a Jimmy Wang Yu film called "Girl with the Thunderbolt Kick." It was a double feature. Something happened during the screening, and the excitement of sneaking into an underage film along with watching the Bruce Lee film left a lasting impression. The interesting thing about "The Big Boss" was that you had to wait about 40 minutes before any action began. You kept waiting to see Bruce Lee's fight scenes, unlike "Enter the Dragon" where the action kicks in right away.

Jeff: Right.

Rick: That was it for me. After that, "Enter the Dragon" was the real eye-opener. The impact it had on me during my first viewing was incredible. I went to see it several times. Did you have a similar experience where it stuck with you, or did you go in and out of being a Bruce Lee fan, or did you become a dedicated fan from that point?

Jeff: After "Five Fingers of Death Aka King Boxer," I wasn't a hard-core fan yet. I was a fan of the film, but not specifically a Bruce Lee fan. When "Fist of Fury (USA Title) AKA Big Boss" came out, it was interesting because the American print of the movie forgot to include Bruce Lee's name in the credits. People in the audience were wondering who he was. It was only when we saw the poster with Bruce Lee's name that we realized who he was. My dad, when asked, confirmed that Bruce Lee was a Kung Fu fighter. His response made me feel proud because, before that, Asian or Chinese people were largely invisible. Now, because of one picture, one man, we were suddenly popular. Even though people criticized "Fist of Fury" aka "The Big Boss" for not having nunchucks or unrealistic stunts, it was similar to how people view "Star Wars." Despite its simplicity compared to "The Empire Strikes Back," the first film holds a special place in the hearts of those who saw Bruce Lee's movies chronologically.

Rick: Did you watch the American print or the Chinese print when you went to the theatre? Was it the American version?

Jeff: Yes, it was the American version. To this day, I tell people that the Peter Thomas soundtrack is my all-time favourite among Bruce Lee movies. I'm sure you remember when the credits appeared in

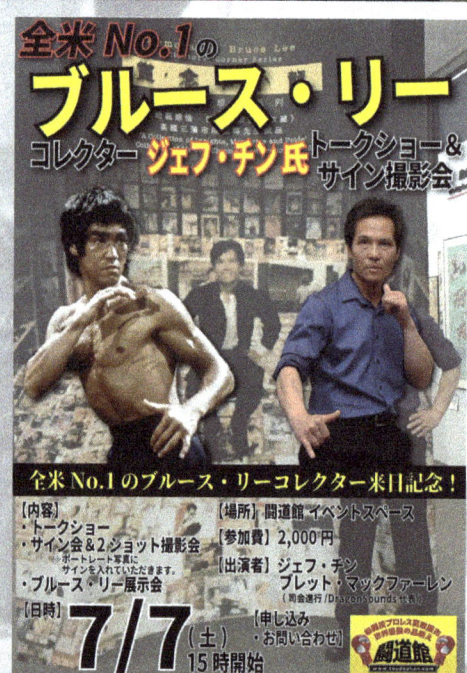

next to a tiger. At the time, the word Kung Fu wasn't well-known in the UK, and it gained popularity mainly with the release of David Carradine's series. I tried to watch "Enter the Dragon" multiple times but couldn't get in. I even went to the back door to listen to the sound effects. Eventually, I bought a ticket for another film, "A Touch of Class" with Glenda Jackson, and as I passed the door, I could hear the movie. I stood there until I was asked to move. My introduction to Kung Fu movies in the UK was "Five Fingers of Death" or "King Boxer." I remember seeing "Deliverance" at the time as well. "The Big Boss" was a significant impact on me, as it was different from what I had seen before. It wasn't like the typical films of the time. It was the beginning of the Kung Fu movie craze, and it was special despite the long wait before Bruce Lee's fight scenes.

Jeff: What a double feature, that sounds exciting.

Rick: It was something. Even though I was eager to see the Bruce Lee film, I saw "Deliverance," which was a good movie, but the lesser-known film "King Boxer" had a significant impact on me because I had never seen anything like it before. This was the beginning of the Kung Fu movie craze, and it felt special, despite "Lo leigh" not having the same charisma as Bruce Lee. I then heard about a cinema near me that was less than glamorous, but they allowed

ed, accompanied by the Peter Thomas score and a cut-out of Bruce Lee doing a flying kick. It's a memory that takes me back to my childhood every time I think about it.

Rick: It's interesting because I think the anticipation had built up by the time I saw "The Big Boss." Magazines were depicting other Bruce Lee films, so we had some knowledge before watching it. By the time I saw it, whether there were credits or not, we already knew Bruce Lee was quite extraordinary. Starting with the credits, though, was somewhat unusual. I had an old print of "Fist of Fury" that had no credits and featured different music. But the anticipation played a significant role. When Bruce Lee started fighting, it was like a boom. When his necklace got ripped off, it felt like an explosive entry. It had a similar impact on me as if I had been sitting there waiting for the action. We were just young kids, not very knowledgeable, and didn't understand much. Bruce Lee was the talk of the school, and people were imitating his moves. Some had seen "Enter the Dragon," but I hadn't. So you had a bit more knowledge going into it, while I went in with limited expectations.

Jeff: It must have been a different experience with that background knowledge

Rick: It kind of helped bit was still very limited at the time compared to today So getting back to "Enter the Dragon".

Jeff: Firstly, "Enter the Dragon" stands out because it features Bruce Lee's actual voice, and it was refreshing to hear him speak. Among all his movies, I believe "Enter the Dragon" showcased the rawest emotion, especially in his expressions and screams. It felt like a step up compared to his previous films. Watching a Chinese actor carry a Hollywood

production was very important for me as an Asian.

Rick: It's funny because I had the "Warner Brothers" radio slots, and they talked about the film before it was released, mentioning Williams, Roper, and introducing Lee Bruce Lee. The moment the film opened, they started giving him top billing and giving more kudos to his name "Bruce Lee Blackmail Hall of Fame." Looking back at the many pictures of Bruce Lee, you can see the different emotions on his face. He had a wide range of expressions. He had the famous scream, and unfortunately, nunchakus were eventually cut from the films due to censorship. In "Way of the Dragon" the film poster was altered to have him use a staff instead of nunchakus. But it was pretty clear that Bruce Lee was not just a martial artist; he was also an actor, influenced by his childhood movies. He had charisma, and this combination allowed him to shine in "Enter the Dragon." I've watched it many times since. I can't say I had this perspective when I first saw it; I was just captivated by his on screen fighting skills. Looking back, Bruce Lee's performances showed various emotions and expressions, making him not just a Kung Fu star but also a talented actor. His X-factor is what set him apart. Were you solely focused on Bruce Lee, or did you continue watching other films, trying to find that unique feeling?

Jeff: Being young, we wanted to watch all the cool Kung Fu films. When Bruce Lee passed away, we sensed that there would never be another like him. Some films not starring Bruce Lee were enjoyable, but the Bruce Lee look-alike movies were awful. After watching a couple of them, my dad, brother, and I decided never to watch them again. The promotions and advertisements for many of these films were deceptive. One that fooled people was "Goodbye, Bruce Lee: His Last Game of Death," which claimed to have a special guest appearance by Kareem Abdul-Jabbar. People went to the theatre with high expectations, thinking they would finally see "Game of Death." However, as soon as the movie started, it was clear that it was another one of those movies.

Rick: In the 70s, many people believed they were watching a Bruce Lee movie when they went to see films like "The Man, the Myth, the Legend" or "Bruce Lee Fights Back from the Grave." Some were disappointed, and it reflected the lack of education about such films back then. I was personally against these movies, although I started to enjoy other films featuring actors like Jackie Chan and Sammo Hung. I had a genuine interest in Hong Kong cinema, and I tried to satisfy it by exploring various films. However, I knew there would never be another Bruce Lee. There have been many look-alikes over the years, but capturing the essence of Bruce Lee remains a challenge. Even now, there's a biopic in the works, but I don't think anyone can truly capture his spirit. When I look back at Bruce Lee's films, each one has a special place in my heart. They bring back distinct memories and feelings, and I appreciate them for different reasons.

Jeff: so In the UK, they cut out the nunchaku scenes when they released "Enter the Dragon" in the UK.

Rick: Not at first, but once they were being used at football matches and in the street in fights the censors decided to cut them from the movies and video release.

Jeff: yes I heard about this through some of my English friends back in the day.

Rick: It's funny how things have evolved. We now have much less trouble with the censors and you can get most films completely uncut being released on many different formats including 4K releases do you still collect Bruce Memorabilia?

Jeff: I stopped collecting memorabilia about ten years ago because the internet made it unnecessary to buy books or magazines, and you could find everything online. You didn't need DVDs anymore since people would upload content to platforms like YouTube. Even if it gets taken down, it pops up again. It saves time because people upload the highlights. Watching uncut footage was great, and we had seen images in magazines of the CART scene. I actually introduced that brothel scene in Inside Kung Fu, as I had a trailer of "The Big Boss" before anyone saw

it. I wrote about it, which inspired someone like Bey Logan to search the archives of Golden Harvest, leading to the discovery of the uncut "Game of Death."

Rick: I was in Hong Kong at the time and Bey showed me the footage i, and it was quite something. As a fan, you're always looking for those new bits of footage, and it was surprising to realise that, even after all these years, the outtakes and unseen footage could still emerge. I watched the Mandarin print of "The Big Boss" with the extended scenes, and it didn't necessarily make it a better film. James Tien was originally meant to be the star, and Bruce Lee seemed to have taken over. Some scenes added context to the story, like the CART scene and the brothel scene. That brothel scene hinted that Bruce Lee was preparing for a fight, like a last fling. It also answered the question of where he got the crisps. You walk away with these little moments, and they make the films more interesting. I also wrote for Bey Logan in 1988 and discussed the scene with the saw in the head. People claimed to see the saw coming down but it's not in any prints. I think it's subliminal; you convince yourself you've seen it.

Jeff: Yes it's always good to see something new especially footage or a rare photo.

Rick: just wondered what your thoughts on "Way of the Dragon Aka Return of the Dragon" Bruce Lee's vision as a director was fascinating, especially in his first directorial debut. He faced difficulties in Rome, as they had no permits and couldn't film in the Coliseum. His creativity and cinematography set him apart. It's possible that Bruce Lee might have transitioned away from Kung Fu films, as they were not as profitable at the time. Once Kung Fu craze had peaked, and the genre didn't make as much money in the cinema anymore, except for big-budget productions like "Crouching Tiger, Hidden Dragon." With so many ways to watch films today, the value of Kung Fu movies has changed.

Jeff: When I finally got to see the original "Way of the Dragon," it was fantastic to see the uncut version with the original screams. That's why I consider "Way of the Dragon" my all-time favourite Bruce Lee movie.

Rick: At what point did you start collecting

Bruce Lee memorabilia? You had that rare magazine that you mentioned that was given to you when you was a small boy, which is very valuable now. What prompted your transition from being a Bruce Lee fan to becoming a dedicated collector?

Jeff: My collecting journey began around 1972, but I didn't collect much until the next year, 1973. During that time, most of the items I purchased were from San Francisco's Chinatown. I had a very modest allowance of $0.75 a week, which meant I could only afford one magazine per week. Back then, those magazines were quite inexpensive. Today, those pre-death magazines are highly sought after, even though their quality is not top-notch. They are prized items for collectors because they were produced during a significant era.

Rick: In the UK, there were some magazines in the local Chinatowns, but they might not have been as frequent as they were in America.

Jeff: Well, I was quite frugal, and I aimed to get the most value for my money. Golden Movie News and similar publications featured some Bruce Lee content, but I only bought the ones that had Bruce Lee on the cover, from cover to cover. My goal at the time was to have the most extensive Bruce Lee collection in my seventh-grade homeroom class. Back then, it was about one-upping each other. People eventually grew out of their Bruce Lee phase, but I stuck with it because of what Bruce Lee meant to me as an Asian American. When my wife and I got married, we bought a small house, and I had a small collection room. However, when we were expecting our first child, we moved in 1991 to a house with a family room that I decided to transform into a Bruce Lee museum or man cave.

Rick: So did you attend the Bruce Lee auctions when you started to become a more serious collector. What was the going price for items back then, like the suit from "Enter the Dragon"?

Eastern Heroes: Bruce Lee Special Vol.2 #3

Jeff: In 1993, I gingerly approached my wife about attending an auction. She thought it sounded expensive since it was in Beverly Hills. She asked what I planned to buy, and I said, "Something small." My intention was to get something from Bruce's movies because those meant the most to me. I didn't want to buy his personal items like ties or shirts he wore at home.

Rick: Which auction was this? Who was donating the items?

Jeff: It was The Bruce Lee Collection Auction (Superior Galleries, 1993). Linda Lee was donating half of the belongings to Shannon and half to Brandon. After Brandon passed away, Linda decided to have an auction to use part of the proceeds for charity in Brandon's name. It was a significant opportunity for Bruce Lee collectors to own items that Bruce Lee wore, touched or used. There were four suits from "Enter the Dragon" at the auction: the blue suit, brown suit, cat suit, and three-piece suit. I initially tried to bid on the cat suit. When it reached around $9,000, my wife grabbed my hand and asked me if I really wanted something like that. We were eventually outbid for the cat suit. However, when the blue suit came up for auction, I won the bid at $7,000, and I managed to outbid Planet Hollywood, which had won the other suits.

Rick: That's quite remarkable. In that era, you knew it was real and authentic.

Jeff: Yes, it was an amazing feeling to have something authentic from Bruce Lee's movies. Back then, you knew you were getting the real deal, which is not always the case these days.

Rick: Was there an auction catalogue with detailed descriptions and photos of the items that were on sale?

Jeff: Yes, there was an auction catalogue that listed around 150 items with detailed descriptions and photographs. The catalogue itself has become a rare collector's item.

Rick: Surprising as there would be Japanese collectors who were well known for being there with plenty of money, so it's surprising that the prices were relatively low.

Jeff: There where very few major Bruce Lee collectors at the auction. The only ones I remember were J.J Goodman, who became the owner of the Black Beauty, and another collector who was Japanese and won a lot of items was Uri Nakamura.

Rick: Yeah, I was very sorry to hear about John passing away last year.
Jeff: Yeah, he had cancer. That's very sad.

Rick: Do you ever look back and think you'd have been happy to acquire more items, given the small fortune you've been sitting on, at today's prices?

Jeff: Well, you have to have a very supportive wife who will allow you to make a purchase like this. Many people might not know that the

week before the auction, I bought another major item. It was the original Chinese Kung Fu book that Bruce Lee wrote, and it was signed. So, by the time I got the book and the blue suit, I didn't have any more money for anything else. In hindsight, if I had a time machine, I'd go back and tell my wife to buy all these items because it would make us very, very rich in the future.

Rick: Often, people start with one item, and that becomes the catalyst for them to start growing their collection. Did that happen to you? Did you begin saving and investing more in these items?

Jeff: one item that skyrocketed was Bruce Lee's cancelled checks. They had a whole stack of them, and they were only charging $495 each. These checks have been going for thousands of dollars.

Rick: Autographs from Bruce Lee can range anywhere from $4,000 to $7,000 or more. Cancelled checks or account foils are sought after because they serve as proof of authenticity. Many of the personal items out there are not genuine.

Jeff: It's unfortunate that even though a cancelled check or a credit card receipt may not look aesthetically pleasing when mounted with a picture of Bruce Lee, it is a guarantee of authenticity. This is important, especially since much of the personal memorabilia out there is questionable.

Rick: Authenticating items can be a real challenge. I've had to authenticate stuff like the nunchakus that Bruce used in "Enter the Dragon". We have to zoom in on a photograph and look for notches and marks to clarify they were genuine because many forged personal items and movie props items were being sold. With today's technology, you can zoom in on a high-res picture to spot marks or details that matched the item. Bruce Lee's signature is one of the easiest to copy. Even Linda could copy it.

Jeff: Well, quite a few checks were signed by Linda in place of Bruce, which was apparent from the signatures looking funny. To make items more valuable, people now want not just Bruce Lee's name but also the Chinese character for Dragon added, which significantly increases their value. However, when non-Asian people attempt to write in Chinese, it can be comical.

Rick: On the Green Hornet items, I've seen him sign his name and then add the Chinese characters after it.

Jeff: Yes, on Green Hornet items, he mostly signed his name. There are some with the Chinese characters, but it can get tricky. People from around the world send me screenshots and ask if they are real or fake. Most of the time, my response is that I hope they didn't buy the items yet.

Rick: When it comes to authenticity, it's often difficult unless you've been to Robert Lee's house or Linda's house, or someone who was there, as there's no definitive way to prove it. Most autographs are terrible, and the most reliable signatures are found on letters.

Jeff: Indeed, the authenticity of items can be a real challenge. Regarding Bob Baker's items, it's unfortunate that they became available for sale. It's a sad situation when such personal memorabilia ends up in the hands of someone who doesn't understand their historical significance from the proceed.

Rick: Yes, the Kids found the cookie Jar after his wife passed, he should have destroyed them or at least tell his wife to benefit from the proceeds

Jeff: yes, at least we knew they were genuine but it's difficult to trust many of the autographs out there, especially when it comes to Bruce Lee's. Unless you have first-hand knowledge or access to people who were directly involved, proving authenticity can be a significant challenge.

Rick: Bruce Lee's signature is widely counterfeited because it's relatively easy to imitate. The best approach to verifying authenticity is through provenance, documents, and historical context.

Jeff: What were your thoughts on Bruce Lee's rumoured substance use in the letters? Based on your knowledge of substance use and its history, it's essential to consider the context and circumstances surrounding it. Bruce Lee wasn't a habitual user but may have had periodic moments of experimentation.

Rick: Bruce Lee's substance use, particularly in Hong Kong, might not have been as frequent as some suggest. It's essential to avoid labelling him as an addict based on incomplete information. His usage could have been more sporadic.

Jeff: I think that, like The Beatles, some of Bruce Lee's best ideas and creations might have come to him during moments when he was influenced by drugs or other factors.

Rick: I spoke to Peter Chan, who trained with Bruce Lee, and he mentioned that Bruce experimented with LSD on occasion, but it wasn't a regular thing. Back then, drugs had a different appeal to people. Bruce, like most people, might have experimented with drugs. It probably didn't affect his abilities. If anything, his back injury and constant thinking about his work might have had more impact.

Jeff: Yes, Bruce Lee had his concerns and worries. He was a human being with his own reality, just like anyone else.

Rick: Absolutely, the 60s and 70s were a different era, and many iconic figures from that time experimented with various things.

Jeff: Some people may have placed Bruce Lee on a pedestal like a god, but it's essential to remember that he was human, with all the complexities and realities that come with being human.

Part two of my interview with Jeff Chinn will be continued in the next Bruce Lee Special December 2023

THE BIG BOSS: RETURN TO THAILAND

Revisiting The Dragon's Den: on 'The Big Boss' Legacy
Rick baker Interviews Matt Routledge on his recent documentary visiting the film location of Bruce Lee's "The Big Boss"

Matt Routledge is a regular contributor to this magazine, and he's also an award-winning filmmaker. However, another string has been added to his bow recently – documentary-maker. When Arrow's Bruce Lee boxset was released in July 2023, it included Matt's latest work – The Big Boss: Return to Thailand. I sat down with him prior to the release of the set to discuss his new piece of work.

RB: Starting at the beginning, how did this project start? Did someone approach you, or was it driven by an ambition of yours? Why a Big Boss documentary? Because it had been done before.

MR: Yes, it had, and John Little did a fantastic job with his. I'll always remember it. One thing I've always wanted to do is a project on Bruce Lee, and I didn't know how I'd be able to do one. So, I thought that maybe I could do an updated 'then and now' project. I'd been to the locations in Thailand, and I'd seen what they looked like. I was planning to make it last only fifteen minutes, but the project grew and grew. When I went over there, I obviously did my bit of filming and found some locations, but I also got lots of interviews with some of the people who were eyewitnesses and saw Bruce. For example, there was someone who worked at the New Wanchai hotel when Bruce was there, providing us with a couple of stories.

RB: I can totally relate to wanting to do something personal about Bruce. The aim is always to find a fresh angle, which I've tried to do in my recent book with Mike and Alan about Enter the Dragon, where we look at the new information coming to light, such as the drugs letters.

MR: Yes, absolutely. I think with this project, it was partially dictated by COVID. I originally wanted to do short location features on The Big Boss, Fist of Fury and Way of the Dragon. Obviously, places got locked up over the pandemic, and I couldn't go over there. Once restrictions slackened,

I felt safest and most confident pursing The Big Boss, because I'd lived in Thailand for a number of years. I already knew about the locations and it felt most feasible to do that. I love the movie – as I do all of them – so decided to go over on a whim. I did a full day of filming on it. I went to the ice factory, where they were very polite and kind, and let me film. I tried to find the original large cutter blades that you see in the film, that were on John Little's documentary, but sadly I couldn't locate them.

RB: They'd have gone straight on eBay…

MR: (laughs) Could have! But I think they'd been destroyed a number of years ago. I didn't find a big, long saw on site anywhere, either! There's a scene where Bruce rings a bell. You know it was an old World War Two bomb that was sawn in half? Well, in the back garden where one of the fight scenes takes place, they've got two that look very similar still hanging up. You'll see it in the documentary. I don't think either one is the one seen in the film, though.

**RB: Thank God that Thailand has preserved some of this! Returning to the documentary, I guess it's very hard to find context, because a lot of people have passed away. Best person I know who's got all the interviews is George Tan. He went out there in the 90s and got them all, but you're never going to see them by the look of it. Anyway, so you went out there on a whim, with no contacts?

MR: I had one contact. He is called Erich Klein, a German ex-pat in Thailand. He helped me to get to some of the locations and arranged a couple of interviews. I had already done a couple myself, but he helped with others.

RB: Who did you meet? Bystanders?

MR: This one doesn't have any famous names. We did try to get Maria Yi to do an interview, but we just couldn't get it over the line, sadly. So, this documentary is more about the Thai people and what they saw. Everyone we have interviewed is Thai, including the caterer at the ice factory. He was literally calling me over while I was filming at the brothel location across the road!

RB: Is that location still in shape?

MR: No, sadly. Because it was a wooden building, it's long gone. They do still have the original blue train station sign that Bruce walks in front of. It's absolutely battered! You can tell it's fifty-plus years old. We filmed there and blended it with the original footage.

RB: As the documentary is part of a film package, does that mean you could use clips to highlight things?

MR: Correct. That's one of the main reasons I gave the film to Arrow. Under their umbrella, Fortune Star, I'm allowed to use the Fortune Star pictures, and the scene to do a direct cross-fade comparison. I got a pile of pictures from Greg Freeman and Andrew Staton to help with that. Having the new remastered footage was amazing. It looks better than it ever has. It basically looks like it was filmed two weeks ago.

RB: It's interesting because me and you came through the 'video scratched tracking error' era. Do you think sometimes that when the print is too clean, it takes away from it? I quite like the retro-looking footage. I know these prints look great on your 4K television, but the studio never filmed or lit it for that quality.

MR: Exactly. I think the Mandarin cut might have that gritty rawness to it because they've been limited in how they can colour

grade it, and how they can alter it, because of limitations in the source material they found it on. Maybe that will give you the flavour of the original feeling. Yeah, I totally get what you mean. Prints are getting so polished and so cleaned up that they're trying to make them look like newer movies.

RB: I don't know if I'm a fan of that. I quite like a 35mm print. The boutique labels are doing quite well with these new releases, but there's something quite nostalgic about the original scratchy footage. For me, anyway!

MR: I always remember the Shaolin Video copies I was paying an arm and a leg for back in the day (laughs).

RB: We were doing some here with Shaolin, and George Tan was in America doing some. Toby and I had the Big Boss print with the original dubbing on. Other dubbing that we heard afterwards doesn't sound quite right.

MR: To be honest, I haven't listened to that one properly, just snippets on YouTube.

RB: Some people prefer subtitles, so it's personal taste really.

MR: One of the things about the documentary is that a lot of the locations in Pak Chong are very near each other. When you go there, you'll be in the Rim Tharn Inn Hotel, where Bruce stayed…

RB: Did you go up to the room?

MR: Yeah, it's still there, you'll see it on the video. I think the swimming pool round the back has gone, where he was rumoured to do a lot of his training, but right behind it, a few hundred yards away, is where the river is, which is the scene where he's sat down with the knives. From there, you cross the road…

RB: What about where they had the fight scene? That's still there, isn't it?

MR: Yes, that's across from the hotel. Wat Siri Samphan Temple. It's probably the most surreal experience you'll have when you go there, because when you walk up to it, you'll get attacked by dogs, like what happened to Bruce in the film.

RB: Really?

MR: Yep, they come up to you, a whole gang, barking like crazy. Someone gave me a tip off that you had to bring a healthy supply of beef jerky with you. But, when you walk onto that grass, it's literally like walking onto the set of the film. It's hardly changed.

RB: You had to do the obligatory flying kick?

THE BIG BOSS
Return to THAILAND

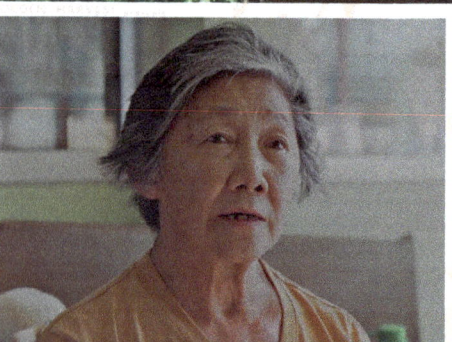

MR: Yeah, I did it. That picture is coming soon. I had to do it. It took a few times though.

RB: I'd have maybe had to photoshop it.

MR: One thing we were lucky about is that the temple is run by some monks, who allowed me to go downstairs. Very few people are allowed. It's where the scene was filmed where Bruce goes down the stairs to chat to the Big Boss. We've got some exclusive footage of that area. What's incredible about that scene is that the nail holes from all of the pictures and hanging ornaments are still on the wall.

RB: That's a lucky find. Nothing lasts forever and that could so easily have been changed.

MR: If Bruce Lee fans want to go on a pilgrimage to these locations while they still survive, they are quite welcome to go to the temple, but they should look to make a donation to the monks. It's a working temple and people should respect that. They're also maintaining a film landmark.

RB: When you set out to make your fifteen-minute feature, did you look at what John Little had done. I guess you covered the same stuff?

MR: I have. There's bits in mine that aren't in his, and bits in his that aren't in mine. Various things have changed over the years, even between my two visits. I found the locations for the James Tien fight, which seems to have been shot in two different places. When he starts fighting, it's on a different road to the reverse angle, which is about two streets away. Another thing in the documentary is about the Nora Miao scene. It divides opinion about where it was shot. The bit where she's on the drinks cart. We present a theory. Locations where we think it might be shot. It has been documented that she said that she filmed it in Bangkok, but we've shown some areas where we think it might have been shot.

RB: What about the bit with the boat?

MR: Yes, we have that. It's on the outskirts distance of each other. Other than the main road outside of the hotel, Pak Chong is a very quiet place. When Bruce went there, it was the rainy season, and it's documented that he and the crew struggled with the storms, but usually, it was very quiet back then.

RB: Has it actually become a pilgrimage for Bruce fans?

MR: Yeah, I think so. There's quite a few people on YouTube who have uploaded videos of their location hunting. It's only a two-to-two-and-a-half-hour car journey from Bangkok, so you can drive down, and stay in the same hotel as Bruce. That's what I

MR: Oh, right.

RB: There may have been some friction. James Tien was already an established star. I would love to have spoken to someone about the relationship between them and ask whether or not it was a bit tense.

MR: I would have loved to have spoken to the stars, but got the sense that they didn't really want to speak about the film anymore, so my focus is on the Thai side. We managed to find one of the policemen from the end of the film. He's quite old now, in his mid-80s. While we were there, calls were made to persuade him to speak to us,

of Bangkok – a place called Phra Pradaeng. Incredibly, a lot of that is all still there. The front where Bruce walks out looks very different now, but it's still a market, so you still get a flavour of the place. Then there's the ice factory. They're doing the same things in there now that they were doing in the film.

RB: I bet places like that really throw you back to the 70s and are full of nostalgia.

MR: Exactly. Like at the temple. I'd advise people to go and visit, they'll have a great time. Everything's in relative walking did. I stayed in the same room that he stayed in. It's got a great view of the back of the hotel.

RB: Amazing! I've just been thinking about James Tien recently, who's quite a shy man in terms of interviews. Toby once had a chance to interview him…

MR: That would have been incredible.

RB: He was with Robert Tai. James Tien said, 'Well, you can, but I'm not necessarily going to say nice things about Bruce Lee.' but he didn't want to do it. In contrast, the catering guy called me across the road. One of the consultants told me that the man said he knew Bruce Lee. It was at the end of a day's filming, and the battery had gone on the camera. So, we had to film the interview quickly on a phone! Luckily someone had a new iPhone with 4K resolution.

RB: Was it just you doing everything?

MR: Yeah. I had a couple of Thai assistants for translation. Erich was helping with arranging interviews. He even managed to get a very brief one with the bus owner's wife. I think the documentary is a nice little accompaniment for the film.

RB: What's the end running time?

MR: 42 minutes. From two days of filming.

RB: That's quite a heavy schedule!

MR: Yeah, I filmed from 5.30 in the morning. We were lucky – everything was scheduled very tightly.

RB: What was your most memorable moment?

MR: The temple. It's iconic. Even the building still looks good. You really get the feeling that you're on the set of The Big Boss.

RB: Have you used any of the soundtracks in your documentary?

MR: We've got the Joseph Koo soundtrack for it, because we had to make sure there weren't any issues over the rights. Arrow advised it. It's a great track!

RB: It's excellent. One of the pieces I can listen to when I'm working is John Barry's Game of Death. Alan Canvan did a great job synching the music to the action.

MR: It's a great soundtrack, too.

RB: With regards to your documentary, at what stage did you join with Arrow? Did they offer any help?

MR: No. I just gave it to them when I was finished. It's a personal project I wanted to do. Giving it to Arrow to include in the boxset is the best way to get it out there, to get it seen.

RB: Did you consider a single release?

MR: No. There are too many rights issues with Fortune Star. I didn't want to tread on anyone's toes. The only way for me to do it properly and to make it look right - to do the footage transitions between the 70s and now - was to release the project through Arrow. Fortunately, they gave me the flexibility to do what I wanted with it. They had a look at the final version, and made a couple of minor comments, but basically it was good to 'go' in the state it was in. For me, it's a privilege to be part of the Bruce Lee boxset. It's probably one of the best releases there's ever been. They've pulled out all the stops.

RB: It's hard to do something new and fresh based around Bruce Lee these days. It's been 50 years.

MR: This has been a passion project for me. When you first watch Bruce Lee films, the ones that strike you straight away are Fist of Fury and Enter the Dragon. They're just so 'in your face'. The fight scenes are amazing, and Bruce is as good as he's ever been. The slow burners were Way of the Dragon and Big Boss. Big Boss has really grown on me over a period of time.

RB: Let's be honest – there's no action for about forty minutes!

MR: Yeah. When I was a kid, I didn't like that. I wanted Bruce to be fighting from minute two! Now I'm older, I like that slow build up.

RB: Exactly. As kids, we were just bothered about the fighting. It's why Game of Death has grown on me so much. I've looked at it more in-depth with Matthew Polly, Ric Meyers and various people, and you see it differently as an 'older' person. How do you rate the Bruce films now?

MR: My favourites were always Fist of Fury and Enter the Dragon, but Big Boss has definitely grown on me. I can't wait to see it on the big screen. It's amazing that all of these cinemas in the UK are showing these Bruce Lee remasters. Bruce is the original and the best. The pinnacle of martial arts cinema.

RB: He had training in acting from being a child, and his martial arts career and life were very short, but he had an X factor.

MR: One of the ladies we interviewed told me something interesting. Apparently, Bruce Lee was already known in Thailand before Big Boss, because they used to watch the Kato show dubbed into Thai on tv. That's what she called it, so I don't know if he was presented as the main star in these cuts, or something. So, he wasn't under the radar!

RB: Has this project inspired you to do any more bonus extras for releases?

MR: I would love to! I have no idea what I'd do, but it would definitely be something I would be interested in.

RB: Thanks very much, Matt! Congratulations on getting your work included on the biggest release for a very long time.

Bruce Lee MEMORABILIA
Collection by Harry McKenzie

李小龍　李小龍

Eastern Heroes: Bruce Lee Special Vol.2 #3

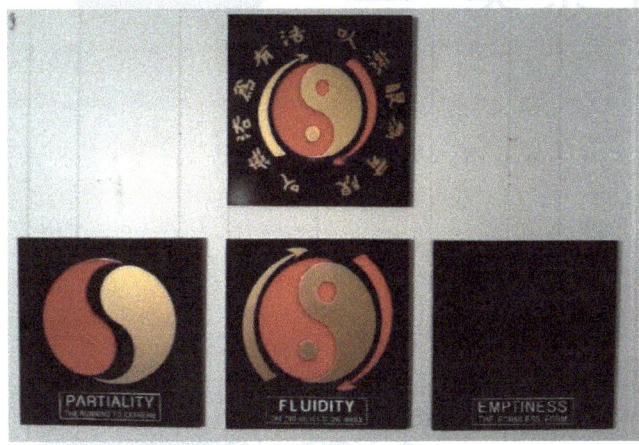

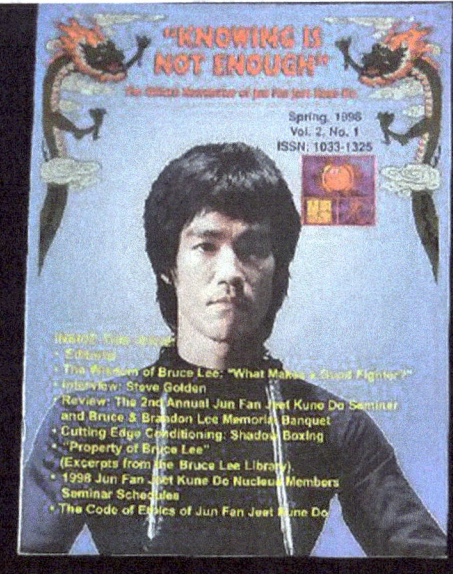

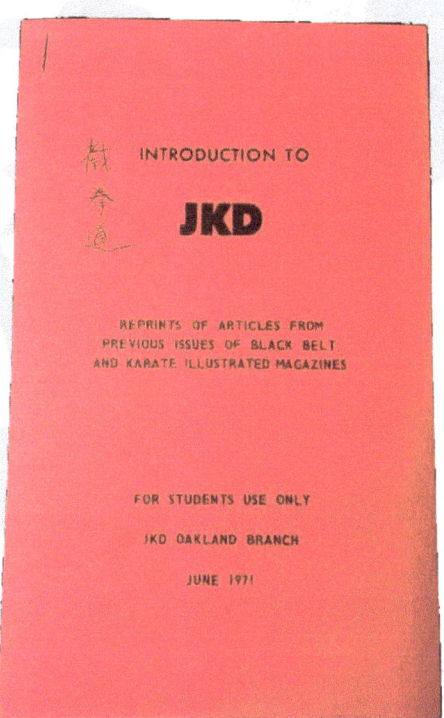
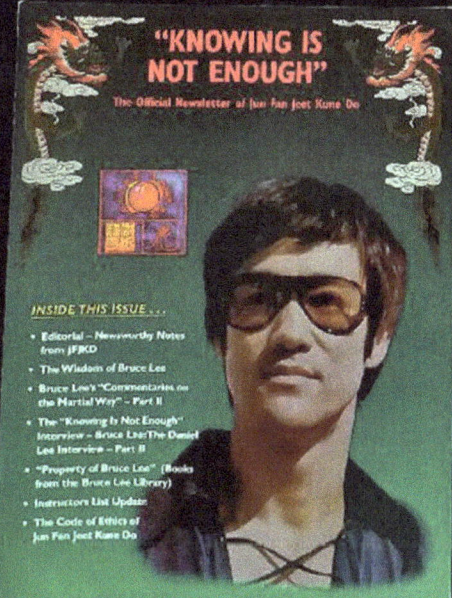

Eastern Heroes: Bruce Lee Special Vol.2 #3

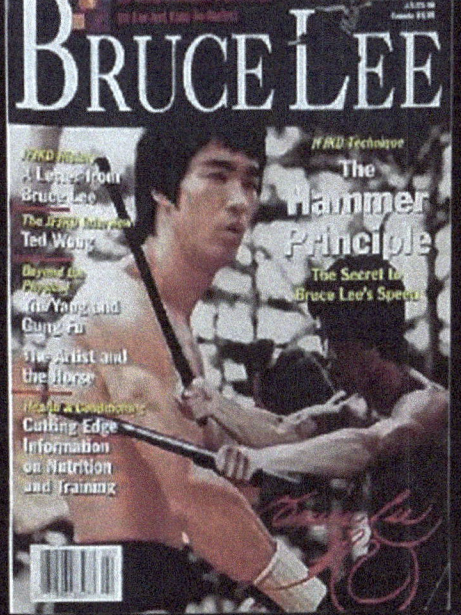

Eastern Heroes: Bruce Lee Special Vol.2 #3

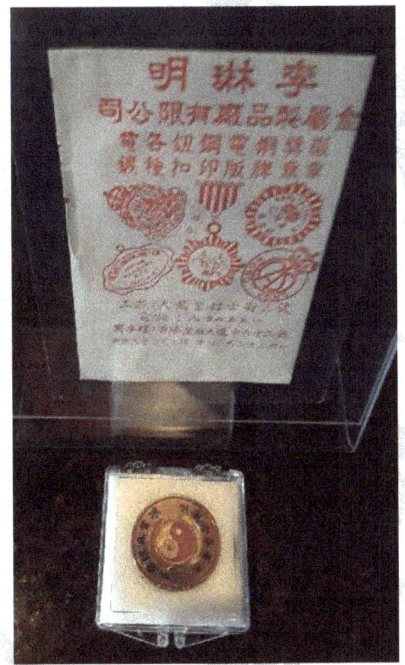

Bruce Lee's Original JKD Pin Given only to his senior Students and a original hand written Envelope from 1968 sent to Taky Kimura when Bruce lived in Culver City, Ca.

I want to first Thank Mr. Ricky Baker and John Negron for making my dream come true and having my collection featured in Eastern Heroes magazine.
Next, I would like to acknowledge the world's Biggest collector Perry Lee from Seattle Washington and the only collector to actually meet Bruce Lee when he was 17 years old for his friendship for the last 25 years and helping me to build my Bruce Lee collection to be what it is today......Thank You my friend, Peace & Brotherhood, Harry McKenzie

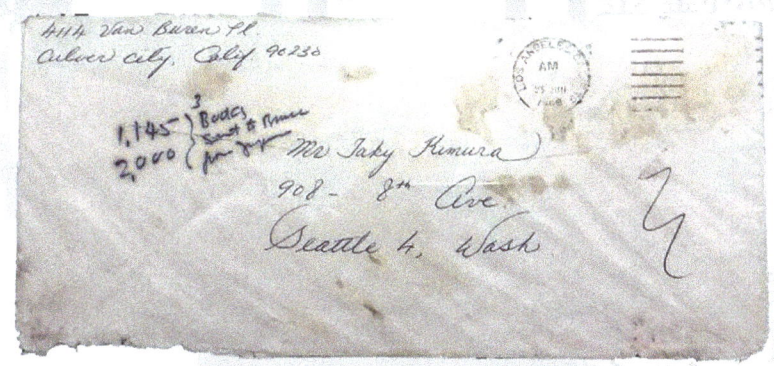

THANK YOU'S

Rick Baker: Editor in Chief

Special Thanks
Simon Pritchard (UK)
Michael Nesbitt (UK)
Steven Morris (Artwork for Fist of Fury cover) (UK)
Thomas Lee (USA)
Johnny Burnett (UK)
Tim Hollingsworth - Designer - Cover & Interior (UK)
Jeff Chinn (USA)
Mike Kelly (USA)
Matt Routledge (UK)
Alan Donkin (UK)
Harry McKenzie (USA)
John Negron (USA)
David Gregory - Severin Films (USA)

www.ingramcontent.com/pod-product-compliance
Lightning Source LLC
Chambersburg PA
CBHW061124170426
43209CB00013B/1668